GRAMMAR REVIEW
FOR THE
TOEFL®

Andrew F. Murphy

A Harvest Test Preparation Book
Harcourt Brace & Company
San Diego   New York   London

Requests for permission to make copies of any part of the work should be
mailed to:
   Permissions Department
   Harcourt Brace & Company
   6277 Sea Harbor Drive
   Orlando, Florida 32887-6777

TOEFL is a registered trademark of Educational Testing Service. This
publication was prepared by Harcourt Brace & Company, which is solely
responsible for its contents. It is not endorsed by any other organization.

Library of Congress Cataloging-in-Publication Data
Jenkins-Murphy, Andrew.
   Grammar review for the TOEFL.
   1. English language—Text-books for foreigners.
2. English language—Examinations, questions, etc.
I. Title.   II. Series.
PR1128.J44   428.2′4   82-2864
ISBN 0-15-600096-2 (pbk.)   AACR2

Printed in the United States of America
H I J K

CONTENTS

What This
Book Will Do
For You

■ **SAVE YOU TIME AND MONEY**

This book will serve as a complete refresher on every aspect of grammar tested in the TOEFL and can dramatically *improve your test scores.*

■ **IMPROVE YOUR TEST-TAKING ABILITY**

Hundreds of exercise items will provide you with an exhaustive survey of the whole range of TOEFL-type grammar and syntax questions. All answers are keyed to *easy-to-read rules, covering grammar, usage, and structure.*

■ **FAMILIARIZE YOU WITH TOEFL-TYPE QUESTIONS**

The questions in the Sample Tests are similar in style, form, and content to those in the actual TOEFL. *They reflect recent administrations of the test.*

■ **ALLOW YOU TO TAKE FOUR PRACTICE TESTS**

The three Sample Tests and the Pre-Test will take you step by step through the Structure and Written Expression portion of the TOEFL. *These tests simulate the actual TOEFL.*

■ EXPLAIN WHY YOUR ANSWERS ARE RIGHT OR
WRONG

The explanations of the answers in each of the Sample Tests
will *improve your understanding of TOEFL questions.*

■ PROVIDE YOU WITH THE MOST THOROUGH REVIEW
OF ENGLISH GRAMMAR AVAILABLE

Each element of English grammar, syntax, and structure is
carefully *explained and then tested in a series of keyed exercises.*

■ ENRICH YOUR UNDERSTANDING OF ENGLISH USAGE

Our unique Usage section specifically attacks those types of
problems that often confront TOEFL students, such as the
difference between *say* and *tell, do* and *make, every one* and
everyone.

■ INCREASE YOUR ABILITY TO USE PUNCTUATION,
CAPITALIZATION, AND ABBREVIATION STYLES
PROPERLY

This guide to current punctuation, capitalization, and abbreviation styles is *an exclusive feature of great value to all
TOEFL applicants!*

Be sure also to see this book's companion volume in the Harvest Test Preparation Series, *How to Prepare for the TOEFL,* for an explanation of the entire test, including Listening Comprehension (Section I) and Reading Comprehension and Vocabulary (Section III). This valuable study aid also includes an audio cassette tape.

How to Use
This Book

Each section of this book can help you achieve a high score on the TOEFL. Read each section carefully, and do the tests and exercises in the order in which they appear.

1. Read the instructions carefully in the section entitled *How to Take the Test*. Pay special attention to the explanation of the types of questions you will find in the Structure and Written Expression section (Section II) of the TOEFL. This review book is primarily designed to help you succeed on that section of the test.

2. Take the *Pre-Test* and score yourself. Check the *Explanatory Answers* and the *Answer Key*. The explanations will direct you to specific rules in the text that will help you understand why your answer was right or wrong.

3. Familiarize yourself with the grammar terms in the *Terminology* section. It may not be necessary to memorize these terms, but you should be able to use this section for reference.

4. Take your time going through the next three sections: *Review of Grammar and Syntax, Punctuation, Capitalization, and Abbreviations,* and *Review of English Usage*. Each of these sections requires careful study. Whenever a rule refers to another rule, take the time to look at that cross-reference. This is important! You need to see how information is related in order to fully understand your new language.

5. Do the exercises for each section and check your answers. These exercises provide you with an excellent opportunity to practice using the grammar

and syntax that are included in the TOEFL questions. The answers to all the exercises are keyed to the rules in that section so you can easily review material you are unsure of.

6. Take the three *Sample Tests*, one per day on three different days. Take these tests under conditions that are similar to those of the actual TOEFL: time yourself, use no books or other aids, and work in a quiet atmosphere. Check the *Answer Key* and the *Explanatory Answers*. Read the explanations for all your answers, whether right or wrong. In this way you will better understand your correct answers and learn from your incorrect answers. Be sure to reread the rules that are keyed to the explanations. By constantly rereading and reinforcing your knowledge, you will attain a high score on the TOEFL.

7. Remember that this review book can also be used as a grammar reference guide in the future.

What Do I Need To Know About The TOEFL?

What Is the TOEFL?

The Test of English as a Foreign Language (TOEFL) measures abilities in English. People whose native language is not English can take this universally accepted test to determine their proficiency in the English language.

Why Take the TOEFL?

Colleges and universities where English is the language of instruction require a TOEFL score. Students seeking admission to undergraduate or graduate programs in such schools are required to submit their TOEFL scores.

Many professions (medicine, nursing, etc.) require licenses. In some cases a TOEFL score may also be required for professional licensing.

Agencies and organizations throughout the world use English as their primary language. Some of them ask job applicants to demonstrate their proficiency in English by taking the TOEFL.

Graduate schools use the TOEFL score as a measure of a student's ability to meet the foreign language requirement for doctoral programs. Scholarship committees use TOEFL scores as part of their screening and awarding processes.

When and Where Is the TOEFL Offered?

The TOEFL is administered once a month at hundreds of test centers in the United States and throughout the world. A list of all current test centers and the dates on which they offer the TOEFL is included in the *TOEFL Bulletin of Information*, a free publication available from TOEFL Services, P.O. Box 6151, Princeton, NJ 08541-6151, USA.

There are two TOEFL testing programs: the Friday Testing Program and the Saturday Testing Program.

If you register for the Friday Testing Program, you will take the TOEFL on a Friday afternoon, you will pay a higher registration fee, and you will have fewer test centers to choose from. The Friday test is given once during each of the following months: March, June, July, September, and December.

If you register for the Saturday Testing Program, you will take the TOEFL on a Saturday morning, you will pay a lower registration fee, and you will have more test centers to choose from. The Saturday test is given once every January, February, April, May, August, October, and November.

Whether you take the TOEFL on Friday or Saturday, at one test center or another, the length and the format of the test (the number and the types of questions) will be the same, as will the administrative procedures. However, the content of the test (the actual questions) will be different. Although some forms of the TOEFL are a little more or a little less difficult than others, the TOEFL scoring scale is adjusted to compensate for these slight differences. Hence all TOEFL scores, past and present, are comparable.

How Do I Register for the TOEFL?

The *TOEFL Bulletin of Information* is a free booklet available to anyone who requests it. Two editions of the *Bulletin,* the United States/Canada edition and the overseas edition, are printed every year. The *Bulletin* lists the dates and locations of all TOEFL tests for that year. It is available at U.S. embassies and consulates, U.S. Information Agency (USIA/USIS) centers, U.S. educational commissions and foundations, and Binational Centers. The *Bulletin* is also available directly from Educational Testing Service (ETS), which administers the TOEFL program. ETS can be reached through TOEFL Services by mail, telephone, fax, cable, or telex:

Mail:	TOEFL Services P.O. Box 6151 Princeton, NJ 08541-6151
Telephone:	609-951-1100
Fax:	609-951-1300
Cable:	EDUCTESTSVC Princeton, NJ
Telex:	5106859596 ETSSCHO A PRIN

Read the *TOEFL Bulletin* carefully. The information it contains is important and may save you time and effort. Each booklet has a registration form, which you should fill out completely and accurately. The registration form is the same for both the Friday Testing Program and the Saturday Testing Program.

When you register for the TOEFL, you must pay the fee for the test in full and in U.S. (or Canadian) dollars. You may not pay in cash; you must pay with a money order or with a check drawn on a U.S. (or Canadian) bank. The money order or check should be made out to ETS-TOEFL.

TOEFL Services should receive your registration form and fee approximately five weeks before the test date you have chosen. The *Bulletin* lists the registration deadline for each test date. If you want to make certain that you get the test date and center of your choice, register early, well in advance of the deadline. Remember that some test centers do not offer the TOEFL every month. Be sure that the center you have chosen is giving the test on the date you wish to take it.

Also be sure to complete your registration form according to the directions in the *Bulletin*. You must print on the form with a medium-soft (No. 2) lead pencil because your marks will be read by a photoelectric scanning machine. If you make a mistake, you must erase your error completely to ensure that it is not read by the machine.

Approximately two weeks before your test, you will receive an admission ticket verifying the date, time, and place of the test. If you have not received the ticket five days before your test date, notify TOEFL Services immediately by telephone, fax, or telex. You must take your admission ticket with you to the test center on the day of the test.

How Do I Prepare for the TOEFL?

Begin your study and preparation process several weeks in advance of the test date (see "How to Use This Book," page 3). Good, solid preparation for the TOEFL is a process that takes time and effort. Four weeks should be sufficient time to prepare yourself thoroughly for the test. If you have only a few days before the test, be sure to take at least one Sample Test. The more time you spend using this text, the better your score will be.

The *TOEFL Bulletin of Information* will also aid you in preparing for the test. It contains an authorized description of the test, a few practice questions, and important information about the procedures at the test center on the test date. In addition, it contains instructions for filling out the admission ticket and the answer sheet that will be used for the test. The *Bulletin* is an important booklet; you should understand it completely.

Before reporting to the test center, attach a passport-size photograph of yourself to the part of your admission ticket marked "photo file record." This photograph must be clear enough to leave no doubt about your identity.

What Do I Take to the Test Center on the Test Date?

On the day of the test, you should take the following items with you to the test center:

- Your admission ticket and your completed photo file record. If, for some reason, you do not have these items but you do have official authorization from TOEFL Services to take the test, be sure to take a recent passport-size photo of yourself to the test center along with your authorization. You will be given a photo file record there, and you will not be admitted to the testing room until after you have completed it.
- Official documentation. You must take your passport contain-

ing your signature and a recognizable photograph, which must be glued or sealed (not stapled) onto the page. Other document requirements vary, so you must consult your *Bulletin* to determine which are needed for your particular center.

- Several sharpened No. 2 (soft-lead) pencils, or a mechanical pencil with soft lead, and an eraser. Some centers supply pencils, but you should be prepared with your own.
- A wristwatch. This is not absolutely necessary, but since each section has a specific time limit, it is wise to monitor your use of time throughout the test.

What Happens When I Get to the Test Center?

Actual testing time for the TOEFL is about 2 hours, but you should expect to be at the test center for 3 to 3½ hours. Be sure to arrive early. When you arrive, your documents will be checked carefully to ensure that you are an officially registered applicant. In addition, the photographs in your official documents will be checked against your appearance. When the admission procedure is completed, you will be allowed to enter the testing room.

Inside the testing room there will be several proctors to guide you to a seat and answer any pretest questions. No one is admitted to the testing room after the test has begun. No food or drink is permitted, and you may not bring any tape or cassette recorders, books, or notes into the testing room. There are no breaks during the test, so be sure to use rest room facilities before entering the room.

What Is the Testing Procedure?

Time is important once the test has begun. Each section has a specific time limit. This period is sufficient to answer all the test questions but does not allow time for daydreaming or spending too much time on any one question. You may work on only one section of the test at a time. The proctors will tell you when to start and when to stop work on each section.

Usually the proctors place applicants according to a predetermined seating plan. Each applicant is seated so that the nearest applicants have differently designed tests. All the applicants in the room are taking the same test at the same time with the same questions, but the arrangement of the questions—the order in which they appear—varies from test to test as they are distributed throughout the room. This means that copying answers from another's answer sheet will do no one any good. The other person's answers may be correct, but they will be in a different sequence, so they will be wrong on the copier's answer sheet.

How Do I Find Out My Test Score?

Soon after the test, score reports are sent to you and to the institutions you indicated on your answer sheet. In some busy seasons, the wait can be a few months, but it normally takes only four to five weeks.

Read the section on score reports in the *Bulletin of Information* carefully. It explains how to use the TOEFL score report request form, how to send or receive additional copies, and how to cancel scores.

You may take the TOEFL as often as you choose. Many applicants take the TOEFL again and again until they score sufficiently high to be accepted by a particular institution.

How Long Will My Test Score Be Valid?

Scores are considered valid for a period of two years, and you may request transcripts of your scores at any time up to two years after your test date. Language proficiency can change in a relatively short time, so the TOEFL office will not send out transcripts of scores that are more than two years old.

What Is a Passing Score on the TOEFL?

There are no passing or failing scores on the TOEFL. Each institution requiring TOEFL scores determines for itself what scores are acceptable. The maximum total score is 677; the minimum, about 200. In general, a score of 600 or above is considered excellent and a score of 400 or below is regarded as poor. Specifically, however, a score is considered good or bad based on the requirements of the institution to which you have applied. Colleges, universities, schools, etc., are free to accept or disregard the following suggested guidelines:

Score Range	*TOEFL Recommended Policy*
550 and above	Admission to graduate or undergraduate programs with no restrictions except: —For those students who score significantly low on one test section (indicating that supplementary work may be needed in order to develop skills in that area).

—For fields where near-native fluency is required (such as journalism). In these cases, a score of 600 may be required.

500–549   Admission to highly technical graduate programs with no restrictions (e.g., engineering, math, physics). Admission to other programs with a limit on the initial academic load and with a required additional English course.

450–499   Admission limited to those who are strong in all other aspects of application. Those admitted should carry a full load of English instruction for a certain time, and their cases should be reviewed on an individual basis.

Below 450   No admission. Applicants in this range are considered unready to begin studies. They should enter a full-time English program before attempting an academic program.

These recommendations assume that applicants meet all the other academic requirements of the programs for which they are applying.

Over the past several years, the average total score (based on thousands of applicants' scores) is a little over 500.

How to Take the Test

FILLING OUT THE ANSWER SHEET

There is a sample answer sheet in the *TOEFL Bulletin of Information*. Read the section entitled "Taking the TOEFL Test," and then practice filling out the sample answer sheet. The part of the answer sheet where you will mark your answers looks like this:

1 Ⓐ Ⓑ Ⓒ Ⓓ
2 Ⓐ Ⓑ Ⓒ Ⓓ
3 etc.

Each problem will have four possible answers: *a, b, c,* or *d.* When you have selected the best choice of the four alternative answers, you will record that choice by marking (darkening) the letter of your choice with a No. 2 (soft-lead) pencil.

EXAMPLE

Rome is a city in

(*a*) Algeria
(*b*) India
(*c*) Italy
(*d*) Mexico   Ⓐ Ⓑ ● Ⓓ

ERASING

The actual test will be graded by a machine; each mark on your answer sheet will be read by the machine. For this reason you should erase all stray (unintentional) marks from your answer sheet.

If you want to change an answer, erase the old mark completely before marking again.

You may *not* write in your test booklet—only the answers on the answer sheet count.

CHECKING YOURSELF

Be sure that you have:

1. Marked an answer for each question, even if you have to guess at a few. There is no penalty for incorrect answers, so be sure to guess even if you are unsure of an answer.

2. Compared your answers to the test booklet questions to ensure that your marked answers correspond to the appropriate questions.

3. Marked only one answer for each question.

4. Erased all stray marks.

PACING YOURSELF

The Structure and Written Expression section of the TOEFL contains 40 questions that you must answer in only 25 minutes. You may spend an average of 38 seconds per question. This is enough time in which to answer each question, but only if you do not lose your concentration. Do not dawdle, or you will run out of time.

GUESSING

You are graded only on your correct answers; no points are deducted for incorrect answers, so you should guess even if you are not sure of an answer.

Answer the questions you know first. Skip over those you don't know, but allow time to come back to them. When you come back to those you've skipped, try to eliminate one or more of the alternative answers and then guess from among the two or three remaining choices.

If you have no idea which is the best choice, then guess at random. Choose a letter and mark that letter for all the questions you are guessing at random. Chances are you'll get at least one out of four, which is better than nothing. Don't worry if you don't know all the answers, but be sure you mark an answer for every question.

If you run out of time while working on a section, just guess and mark your chosen letter for all those questions you haven't answered in that section. TOEFL rules state that you may not return to a section after the entire group has gone on to a new section.

THE TEST BOOK

When you finish taking the TOEFL, your test book will be collected, along with your answer sheet. *Make no marks in your test book* while you're taking the test. Marking up your test book in any way, including underlining and note taking, is strictly forbidden.

FORMAT AND DIRECTIONS

Familiarize yourself with all the directions for the TOEFL. When you take the actual test, you will find that time for reading the directions is included in the total time allotment. Thus, the less time you have to spend reading directions, the more time you will have to work on answering questions.

The Sample Tests in this book are exactly like the actual TOEFL in format and organization. TOEFL questions are not repeated from one test to another, but the format and organization of the test remain the same.

SECTION II OF THE TOEFL: STRUCTURE AND WRITTEN EXPRESSION

Section II consists of Part A and Part B.

Part A is designed to measure your ability to recognize language that is appropriate for standard written English. This means you will be tested on your knowledge of English grammar, word order, usage, sentence structure, etc.—all the elements that constitute proper or accepted use of a language.

In this part there are usually 15 questions, each consisting of an incomplete sentence. The missing word or phrase is designated by a blank (_____). Four alternatives for completing the sentence are listed below the sentence. You are to choose the one word or phrase marked (a), (b), (c), or (d) that best completes the sentence. Then, find the number of the question on your answer sheet and mark the letter of your answer. Be sure to blacken or darken the oval that corresponds to your answer so that the letter inside cannot be seen. You will have 10 minutes to complete this part of the test.

Here are some examples of the type of question in Part A:

EXAMPLE 1.

Giles has already left for Spain, _____ ?

(a) isn't it
(b) has he
(c) doesn't he
(d) hasn't he

EXAMPLE 2.

Mrs. Quartermaine has lived across the hall from us _____ .

(a) for four years
(b) since four years ago
(c) four years ago
(d) since four years

EXAMPLE 3.

The applicants walked _____ the room and immediately sat down.

(a) in
(b) into
(c) with
(d) on

In some of these types of problems, the answer can come from knowledge of grammar alone. In Example 1, the construction of the sentence calls for a tag question, or tag ending. This is a short confirmation of some already known fact that is presented in question form. Answer (a) uses the pronoun *it*; Giles, however, is a *he*, so we can eliminate (a). Tag endings call for the opposite of the form used in the main clause; thus, affirmative statements require negative tag endings. Answer (b) is stated affirmatively, so we can eliminate it. The auxiliary verb in a tag ending should be the same as that in the main clause, so we can eliminate (c). Answer (d) is correct. For further review and study, see section 94 in the grammar review portion of the text.

In Example 2, only answer (a) is acceptable. *Since* must be used with a term that includes a date, such as *since August* or *since 1980*. Thus, we can eliminate (b) and (d). The use of the present perfect tense eliminates the possibility of using *ago* [choice (c)], which is only used with the past tense. See grammar section 78 for exact time patterns using *since*, *ago,* and *for.*

In Example 3, you must know the definitions and usage of prepositions. One cannot walk *with* or *on* a room, thus eliminating choices (c) and (d). *In* means "within," expressing no action; thus, (a) is eliminated. *Into* expresses action from without to within; only (b) is appropriate. See grammar section 189.

Part B further measures your ability to recognize language that is appropriate for standard written English. It measures your mastery of important structural and grammatical points and your understanding of an acceptable style of writing English. This part is sometimes referred to as the written expression or writing ability portion of the test.

All the questions in this part of the test will be multiple-choice questions, like those in all the other sections. You will not be asked to write a composition.

In this part there are usually 25 questions, each consisting of a sentence in which four words or phrases are underlined. Each underlined word or phrase is marked (a), (b), (c), or (d). You are to choose the one word or phrase that would *not* be acceptable in standard written English, that is, the word or phrase that should be corrected or rewritten. Find the number of the question on your answer sheet and mark the letter of the answer you have chosen as unacceptable. You will have 15 minutes to complete this portion of the test.

Here are a few examples of the type of question in Part B:

EXAMPLE 4.

    When she complained of <u>too</u> <u>many</u> noise, the neighbor <u>said</u>
                                                a   *b*   *c*
    he <u>would turn</u> his stereo down.
            d

EXAMPLE 5.

    It was <u>on</u> June 26, 1945, <u>that</u> <u>they</u> signed the charter of
                a   *b* *c*
    <u>the United Nations.</u>
            d

EXAMPLE 6.

Just <u>among</u> the two of us, I think they <u>should have</u> waited
　　　　a　　　　　　　　　　　　　　　　*b*

a <u>few</u> years to <u>get married</u>.
　c　　　　　　*d*

In Example 4, term (*b*) is unacceptable in carefully written English. *Many* is used with plural countable nouns, such as *many sounds*. *Much* is preferred with abstract and noncountable nouns such as *noise*. The sentence should read: "When she complained of too much noise, the neighbor said he would turn his stereo down." See grammar section 145.

In Example 5, term (*c*) is unacceptable. Pronouns must refer to antecedents clearly; *they* does not refer to any particular antecedent. If a sentence does not have an active subject, it would be better to write it in the passive voice: "It was on June 26, 1945, that the charter of the United Nations was signed." See grammar section 252.

In Example 6, term (*a*) is unacceptable. *Among* is used to compare three or more items; *between* is used to compare two items. The sentence should read: "Just between the two of us, I think . . . ." See grammar section 180.

Pre-Test

Pre-Test

You are now ready to take the Pre-Test. Use the answer sheet on the facing page to record your answers to the questions. Take the test under simulated TOEFL conditions: Allow 10 minutes for Part A and 15 minutes for Part B; have no books or other aids near you; use a soft-lead pencil to mark your answers on the answer sheet; find a quiet place where noises will not distract you. When you have finished the entire Pre-Test, check your answers against the Explanatory Answers that begin on page 26.

Good luck!

Pre-Test Answer Sheet

When you have chosen your answer to any question, blacken the corresponding space on the answer sheet below. Make sure your marking completely fills the answer space. If you change an answer, erase the previous marking completely.

For convenience, you may wish to remove this sheet from the book and keep it in front of you during the test.

1 Ⓐ Ⓑ Ⓒ Ⓓ	11 Ⓐ Ⓑ Ⓒ Ⓓ	21 Ⓐ Ⓑ Ⓒ Ⓓ	31 Ⓐ Ⓑ Ⓒ Ⓓ
2 Ⓐ Ⓑ Ⓒ Ⓓ	12 Ⓐ Ⓑ Ⓒ Ⓓ	22 Ⓐ Ⓑ Ⓒ Ⓓ	32 Ⓐ Ⓑ Ⓒ Ⓓ
3 Ⓐ Ⓑ Ⓒ Ⓓ	13 Ⓐ Ⓑ Ⓒ Ⓓ	23 Ⓐ Ⓑ Ⓒ Ⓓ	33 Ⓐ Ⓑ Ⓒ Ⓓ
4 Ⓐ Ⓑ Ⓒ Ⓓ	14 Ⓐ Ⓑ Ⓒ Ⓓ	24 Ⓐ Ⓑ Ⓒ Ⓓ	34 Ⓐ Ⓑ Ⓒ Ⓓ
5 Ⓐ Ⓑ Ⓒ Ⓓ	15 Ⓐ Ⓑ Ⓒ Ⓓ	25 Ⓐ Ⓑ Ⓒ Ⓓ	35 Ⓐ Ⓑ Ⓒ Ⓓ
6 Ⓐ Ⓑ Ⓒ Ⓓ	16 Ⓐ Ⓑ Ⓒ Ⓓ	26 Ⓐ Ⓑ Ⓒ Ⓓ	36 Ⓐ Ⓑ Ⓒ Ⓓ
7 Ⓐ Ⓑ Ⓒ Ⓓ	17 Ⓐ Ⓑ Ⓒ Ⓓ	27 Ⓐ Ⓑ Ⓒ Ⓓ	37 Ⓐ Ⓑ Ⓒ Ⓓ
8 Ⓐ Ⓑ Ⓒ Ⓓ	18 Ⓐ Ⓑ Ⓒ Ⓓ	28 Ⓐ Ⓑ Ⓒ Ⓓ	38 Ⓐ Ⓑ Ⓒ Ⓓ
9 Ⓐ Ⓑ Ⓒ Ⓓ	19 Ⓐ Ⓑ Ⓒ Ⓓ	29 Ⓐ Ⓑ Ⓒ Ⓓ	39 Ⓐ Ⓑ Ⓒ Ⓓ
10 Ⓐ Ⓑ Ⓒ Ⓓ	20 Ⓐ Ⓑ Ⓒ Ⓓ	30 Ⓐ Ⓑ Ⓒ Ⓓ	40 Ⓐ Ⓑ Ⓒ Ⓓ

Pre-Test

PART A (15 questions; 10 minutes)

In Part A each problem consists of an incomplete sentence. Four words or phrases, marked (*a*), (*b*), (*c*), (*d*), are given beneath the sentence. You are to choose the one word or phrase that best completes the sentence. Then on your answer sheet, find the number of the problem and mark your answer.

1. Who will get your job when you leave is _____ .

   (*a*) anybodys guess
   (*b*) anybody's guess
   (*c*) the guess of someone
   (*d*) anybody else's guess

2. Are you sure you don't have _____ advice to give me? I really need _____ .

   (*a*) any . . . any   (*c*) some . . . any
   (*b*) an . . . some   (*d*) any . . . some

3. They wished that he _____ to accompany them last night, but he couldn't.

   (*a*) were able   (*c*) was able
   (*b*) had been able   (*d*) has been able

4. Nora always _____ she _____ live to be 100 years of age.

   (*a*) said . . . will   (*c*) said . . . would
   (*b*) says . . . would   (*d*) says . . . wouldn't

5. The drum and bugle corps _____ when we reached the reviewing stand.

   (*a*) already passed
   (*b*) had already passed
   (*c*) has already passed
   (*d*) had been passed

6. The basketball team had a decided advantage with its two _____ guards.

    (a) six foot   (c) six feet
    (b) six-foot   (d) six-feet

7. She showed us several types of floral arrangements and then pointed to one and said, "_____ is my favorite."

    (a) These kind   (c) This kind
    (b) Those kind   (d) That kinds

8. Barbara Tuchman wrote extensively about _____ Maginot Line and its role prior to World War II.

    (a) the   (c) an
    (b) a   (d) (no article)

9. The slain president was _____ leader in his part of the world.

    (a) the uniquest   (c) a unique
    (b) a most unique   (d) the most unique

10. They promise to come _____ they can find a babysitter.

    (a) except   (c) providing
    (b) without   (d) provided

11. _____ Perry wanted to move to Ann Arbor.

    (a) When he saw how good Michigan's program was,
    (b) He saw how good Michigan's program was, and
    (c) He saw how good Michigan's program was
    (d) When he saw how good Michigan's program was.

12. I don't think that one person can do the job; we need three people to do it: _____

    (a) an administrator, a technician, and a mentor.
    (b) an administrator, technician, and mentor.
    (c) an administrator-technician-mentor.
    (d) an administrator, technician, mentor.

13. She answered, "I'm busy tonight. I can't go." He then asked _____

    (a) when she can go.   (c) when she could go.
    (b) when could she go.   (d) when she can go.

14. They advised us _____ until the crisis was over.

    (a) to postpone leaving   (c) to postpone to leave
    (b) postponing leaving   (d) postpone to leave

15. Julia didn't drive her car today, _____

    (a) but Andrea did too.   (c) and Andrea did.
    (b) but so did Andrea.   (d) but Andrea did.

PART B (25 questions; 15 minutes)

Each problem in Part B consists of a sentence in which four words or phrases are underlined. The four underlined parts of the sentence are marked (a), (b), (c), (d). You are to identify the one underlined word or phrase that should be corrected or rewritten. Then on your answer sheet, find the number of the problem and mark your answer.

16. <u>Whose</u> glasses case is <u>this</u>? Is it <u>your's</u>? No, I think it's <u>hers</u>.
      a   *b*   *c*   *d*

17. Last night <u>at</u> dinner, Gina told <u>us</u> that she <u>wants</u> <u>to get</u> her
            a   *b*   *c*   *d*
master's degree in social work.

18. Everything you have written in your series of articles <u>make</u>
                                                a
sense, <u>but</u> I don't think <u>anyone</u> will <u>pay attention</u>.
       b   *c*   *d*

19. An <u>extension</u> tube <u>to water the high plants</u> was placed <u>on</u>
          a   *b*   *c*
our regular <u>can</u>.
         d

20. Bernice lived in <u>New Orleans Louisiana</u> <u>until</u> she <u>was</u> 9 years
                   a   *b*   *c*
<u>old</u>.
d

21. I can't tell <u>by</u> her accent, but I think <u>she</u> <u>said</u> <u>she</u> was <u>of</u>
          a   *b*   *c*   *d*
Czechoslovakia.

22. You better take advantage of this offer while you can.
      a   *b*   *c*   *d*

23. She's wearing that new cotton sweater I gave herself today,
           a   *b*   *c*   *d*
    isn't she?

24. I often have difficulty solving those sort of solid geometry
      a   *b*   *c*
    problems, don't you?
              d

25. When one opens an account at Dominion Savings and Loan,
            a   *b*
    you can get the first set of checks for free.
     c   *d*

26. The geologist told her student that she would be spending
                          a *b*   *c*
    the night sleeping "under the stars."
           d

27. While we were working on the theorem, Dr. van Eyck said,
          a   *b*   *c*
    "Sometimes I wish I was Einstein."
               d

28. "I stealed the necklace, but I didn't mean to hurt her," the
     a   *b*   *c*   *d*
    thief cried.

29. Neil always said that he shouldn't have smoked as much as
       a   *b*   *c*
    he did smoke.
      d

30. You haven't already loaned your copy of the nursing journal
            a   *b*
    to Vicki, did you?
      c   *d*

31. I think we must to register each year in January at the local
             a   *b*   *c* *d*
    post office.

32. <u>Stand closely</u> to the stage door <u>so that</u> we <u>can see</u> her <u>when</u>
    a   b   c   d
    she comes out.

33. We're considering <u>switching</u> our heating system <u>from</u> oil to
                       a   b
    gas; we <u>think</u> it will cost <u>fewer</u> money that way.
            c   d

34. This cookie jar is <u>emptier</u> today <u>than</u> it was yesterday. <u>Who's</u>
                       a   b   c
    been <u>eating</u> the cookies?
         d

35. Ms. Winfield <u>always</u> told us that <u>the</u> hard work was <u>its</u> <u>own</u>
                 a   b   c   d
    reward.

36. The Nobel committee decided to wait <u>as far as</u> <u>the end of</u> the
                                        a   b
    current peace talks before <u>choosing</u> this <u>year's</u> winner.
                               c   d

37. <u>Mrs.</u> D'Amico had <u>so much</u> trouble getting <u>in</u> the car that we
    a   b   c
    had <u>to help</u> her.
        d

38. They always <u>change</u> their <u>bed linens</u> on Sundays, <u>since</u>
                a   b   c
    <u>yesterday</u> they were so busy that they forgot.
    d

39. She asked <u>us</u> <u>to mail</u> her <u>from Peru</u> <u>some</u> alpaca sweaters.
             a   b   c   d

40. I <u>told</u> the mechanic to <u>say</u> me the estimated cost <u>before</u> she
      a   b   c
    started <u>to repair</u> my car.
            d

STOP! End of TOEFL Pre-Test

Pre-Test: Answer Key

1. *b*	11. *a*	21. *d*	31. *a*
2. *d*	12. *a*	22. *a*	32. *a*
3. *b*	13. *c*	23. *d*	33. *d*
4. *c*	14. *a*	24. *b*	34. *a*
5. *b*	15. *d*	25. *c*	35. *b*
6. *b*	16. *c*	26. *b*	36. *a*
7. *c*	17. *c*	27. *d*	37. *c*
8. *a*	18. *a*	28. *a*	38. *c*
9. *c*	19. *b*	29. *d*	39. *c*
10. *d*	20. *a*	30. *d*	40. *b*

Pre-Test: Explanatory Answers

Numbers in parentheses after each explanation refer to the corresponding rules in this book's review sections on grammar and syntax, punctuation, and usage.

1. (*b*) Choice (*b*) is the correct idiom for this construction. The phrase requires an apostrophe. Choice (*a*) is eliminated because it has no apostrophe; (*c*) and (*d*) are correct English, but inappropriate in this sentence. (**18**)

2. (*d*) *Any* or *some* could be used in the first clause, but only *some* is acceptable in the second, which is an affirmative statement. All other choices are grammatically unacceptable. (**40**)

3. (*b*) The past perfect tense is used to suggest past action in subjunctive mood constructions that express wishes. Choice (*a*) uses the past tense, which is used to suggest present action in this type of construction (They wish that he were able to accompany them tonight); (*c*) and (*d*) are unacceptable verb forms for the subjunctive mood. (**65**)

4. (*c*) In a complex sentence, the tense of the main clause verb determines the tense of the dependent clause verb. Since the main clause verb (*said*) is in the past tense, the past tense form *would* is used. (**92**)

5. (*b*) The past perfect tense is needed to show that one event in the past (the passing of the corps) took place before another event in the past (when we reached the stand). Choices (*a*) and (*c*) use the wrong tenses; (*d*) uses the passive voice. (**79**)

6. (*b*) Compound adjectives that precede nouns use hyphens, and adjectival forms of measurement are singular, as in "a three-mile race." All the other forms are unacceptable. (**137; 282**)

7. (c) Since she pointed to only one arrangement, the adjective and noun construction should be singular, as is indicated by the verb *is*. Choices (a), (b), and (d) all have some plural form. (**147**)

8. (a) *The* is used to refer to particular nouns. Choices (b) and (c) refer to unspecified nouns; (d) is used when nouns are not qualified. (**171–174**)

9. (c) By definition, *unique* means "one of a kind"; thus, it is absolute, not comparable; there can be no degrees of uniqueness. (**166**)

10. (d) Only *provided* is a conjunction; thus, it is the only choice that can introduce the clause. (**193**)

11. (a) Since the first thought in this sentence depends on the second thought, it should be in a subordinate clause; thus, choice (a) is correct. Choice (b) would make the two clauses inappropriately equal; (c) uses no punctuation and no conjunction to join the two thoughts; (d) uses a fragment as a sentence. (**206–208; 228**)

12. (a) Only (a) clearly expresses the three different people. Choices (b) and (c) indicate one person; (d) is grammatically unacceptable. (**175; 232**)

13. (c) Only (c) correctly uses the tense and form for reporting discourse indirectly: present becomes past, and questions become statements. (**253a; 256b**)

14. (a) Only (a) is acceptable: *advise* is followed by an infinitive, and *postpone* is followed by a gerund. (**123; 125**)

15. (d) Only (d) expresses opposite situations correctly. Choices (a) and (b) start with *but* (expressing contradiction), but then inappropriately use similarity words, *too* and *so*; (c) uses the correct verb form, but since one person drove and the other didn't, *and* is inappropriate for indicating contrast. (**96**)

16. (c) Possessive personal pronouns never take apostrophes. Thus, "Whose glasses case is this? Is it yours? No." (**18; 22c**)

17. (c) When someone is quoted indirectly, the present tense changes to the past. Gina probably said, "I *want* to get . . . ," but since she is being quoted indirectly, the tense must change. Thus, ". . . told us that she wanted to get . . . ." (**253**)

18. (a) *Everything* is a singular subject pronoun; it requires a singular predicate. Thus, "Everything . . . makes sense, but . . . ." (**35; 249**)

19. (b) This infinitive phrase is dangling; it *must* refer to some part of the sentence, even if the sentence has to be re-formed and rewritten. Thus, "We placed an extension tube on our regular can in order to water the high plants." (**222**)

20. (*a*) *Louisiana* is functioning as an appositive, giving additional information about *New Orleans* (where it is); thus, it must be set off by commas from the rest of the sentence. Thus, "Bernice lived in New Orleans, Louisiana, until she . . . ." (**200; 270**)

21. (*d*) The correct preposition for indicating a person's place of birth or residence is *from*. Thus, ". . . said she was from Czechoslovakia." (**190g**)

22. (*a*) The auxiliary verb *had better* is used to express advisability. Thus, "You'd better take advantage of . . . ." (**103**)

23. (*d*) Reflexive pronouns reflect or emphasize, but they may not substitute for pronoun objects. Thus, ". . . sweater I gave her today . . . ." It would, however, be acceptable to say "She herself is wearing . . ." or "She made the sweater herself." (**26; 28; 29**)

24. (*b*) *Those* is a plural demonstrative pronoun; *sort* is a singular noun. One of them must change to make the sentence grammatically correct. Thus, ". . . that sort of solid geometry problem . . ." or ". . . those sorts of solid geometry problems . . . ." Note that *problem* must agree too. Because *problems* is already plural in this sentence, *sort* must change to *sorts*. (**33; 34**)

25. (*c*) *You* should only be used when addressing a specific person or persons; the indefinite *one* is the appropriate pronoun when the meaning is "someone" or "anyone." *One* is used correctly in the first clause, and it should be used in the second. Thus, "When one opens . . . , one can get . . . ." (**39**)

26. (*b*) The pronoun could refer to the geologist or to her student. As the sentence is written, the reference is not clear; it should be rewritten. Thus, "The geologist said to her student, 'You'll be spending the night under the stars,' " or "The geologist said to her student, 'I'll be spending the night under the stars.' " (**46; 252**)

27. (*d*) The verb *be* takes the form *were* in the past tense in a subjunctive mood sentence. A *theorem* is an idea that is assumed to be true. (**63**)

28. (*a*) The past tense of *steal* is *stole*. (**72**)

29. (*d*) There is no valid reason for repeating the main verb in this construction which uses *as . . . as*. Thus, ". . . shouldn't have smoked as much as he did." (**100**)

30. (*d*) Affirmative tag endings/questions are used after negative statements; the same auxiliary that appeared in the statement is used. Thus, "You haven't already loaned . . . have you?" (**94**)

31. (*a*) *Must* is never followed by an infinitive. Thus, "I think we must register each year . . . ." (**113**)

32. (*a*) The correct form of the adverb in this construction is *close*. Thus, "Stand close to the stage door . . . ." (**130**)

33. (d) *Fewer* is used with countable nouns; *less* is used with noncountable nouns. Thus, ". . . it will cost less money that way." (143)

34. (a) *Empty* is an absolute term; a thing cannot be more or less empty. Thus, "This cookie jar is more nearly empty today than . . . ." or "This cookie jar is almost empty today; who's been . . . ." (166)

35. (b) No article is used with noncountable nouns. Thus, ". . . told us that hard work . . . ." If the term *hard work* had been followed by modifiers, this type of construction would have been acceptable: ". . . told us that the hard work we were destined for was its . . . ." (171; 174)

36. (a) The phrase *as far as* is used to express physical distance; *until* is used to express time. Thus, ". . . decided to wait until the end of . . . ." (182)

37. (c) *In* expresses no action, whereas Mrs. D'Amico is moving from outside of the car to inside it; *into* expresses the action of movement. Thus, ". . . so much trouble getting into the car . . . ." (189)

38. (c) Subordinate conjunctions join dependent clauses to independent ones. In this sentence, however, both clauses are independent; that is, each can stand alone as a sentence. In a construction such as this, a coordinate conjunction should be used to connect the thoughts of equal rank. Thus, ". . . their bed linens on Sundays, but yesterday they . . . ." *Bed linens* are sheets, pillowcases, etc. (195; 196)

39. (c) This phrase is misplaced; she doesn't want us to mail *her* from Peru, she wants us to mail *some sweaters* from Peru. Adverbial modifiers must not come between predicates and their direct objects. Thus, "She asked us to mail her some alpaca sweaters from Peru." (214)

40. (b) *Say* is inappropriate in this construction because the person spoken to is mentioned (*me*), and the verb is followed by an indirect object (*me*). Thus, "I told the mechanic to tell me . . . ." (Usage: **say, tell**)

Terminology:
A Review and
Reference List

Terminology: A Review and Reference List

Active voice: The verb form that indicates that the subject of the sentence is doing or causing the action or effect that is expressed by the verb.

> Hunter cooked a meal.

Adjective: A word that describes, modifies, or limits the meaning of a noun, pronoun, or noun phrase.

> *hot* water   *altered* states   *little* boys

Adverb: A word that qualifies or describes the meaning of a verb, an adjective, or another adverb. It can tell how, where, when, how often, or to what degree.

> *softly, now, here, frequently, not*   She *frequently* sang *softly*.

Affirmative: Describing a word or sentence that is represented and asserted as true. The opposite of negative.

> Yes, I live in the U.S.

Antecedent: A noun, pronoun, or noun phrase that a pronoun replaces and refers to. (In this sentence, *Dick* is the antecedent, *he* is the pronoun.)

> *Dick* was here yesterday, but today he isn't.

Apostrophe: A mark (') that indicates the omission of a letter or letters in a contraction, or that notes possession.

> isn't   they're   two year's time   Fred's bank

Appositive: A word or phrase that explains or further identifies a noun or pronoun. An appositive usually follows immediately upon the noun or pronoun to which it is in apposition.

> Bill, *a husband and father*, is president of our club, *the Business Leaders of Pennsylvania Avenue*.

Article: A limiting adjective. *The* is definite; *a* and *an* are indefinite.

> *the* book   *a* book   *an* open book

Auxiliary verb: A verb that accompanies the main verb of a clause or sentence and helps express its tense, mood, or voice.

> It *could* not *be* helped.   They *will have* seen her already.

Capital: Describing an upper-case letter, such as *A* or *P*; lower-case letters are *a* and *p*.

Case: The relationship of nouns, pronouns, and adjectives to the other words in the sentence, as indicated by their position in the sentence.

Clause: A group of related words with both a subject and a predicate.

> When I see her . . .   Drive slowly.

Collective noun: The name of a collection, group, or set of persons, places, things, etc.

> team, jury, audience

Colon: A mark (:) that indicates that something, often a list, is to follow.

> The new Fords are available in the following colors: red, green, etc.

Comma: A mark (,) that indicates a short pause and a separation of ideas or elements in a phrase, clause, or sentence.

> Yes, Jane, you'll need food, clothing, and money.

Common noun: A noun that names the kind or class of person, place, thing, etc.

> woman   giraffe   heat   grass

Comparative: Describing the degree of comparison of adjectives or adverbs that relates two items to each other.

> She spoke *louder* and *more distinctly* than her brother did.

Complement: A word or phrase that completes the meaning of the verb in a clause or sentence. The construction of the predicate can be completed by the complement.

> She is *a manager.*
> This winter will be *long and cold.*
> He asked *if he could miss practice today.*

Complex sentence: A sentence with one independent clause and one or more dependent clauses.

> When the snow melts, we'll plant crops.

Compound: Referring to two equal elements that have been joined in a sentence.
> **compound subject:** *Harry and Al* own a restaurant.
> **compound verb:** They *live and work* here.
> **compound adjective:** a *broad-shouldered* man; the *fire-resistant* cloth
> **compound sentence:** *She is an optometrist and he is an optician.*
> (A compound sentence has two or more coordinate independent clauses, usually joined by a conjunction.)

Conjugation: A systematically arranged listing of all the forms of a verb corresponding to tense, voice, mood, number, person, and gender.

Conjunction: A word that connects or joins two or more words or ideas, showing the relationship between them.

> Millie *and* Jo are old, *but* they are lively *and* young at heart.

Conjunctive adverb: A word that modifies the clause that it introduces and that joins two independent clauses. It functions as both an adverb and a conjunction.

> Nelly didn't finish her botany course; *instead*, she took a job and moved to Los Angeles.

Consonant: Any of the 26 letters of the alphabet except *a, e, i, o,* and *u.*

Coordinate conjunction: A conjunction that connects two equal and identically constructed parts.

> *and, but, for, or, nor, yet*

Correlative conjunction: A conjunction that connects items of equal rank and similar form that are used in pairs. It shows their reciprocal or complementary relationship.

> *Neither* Mr. Harris *nor* Ms. Garcia is here.

Countable nouns: Nouns that can be totaled, numbered, or counted.

> a book   ten books

Declension: A systematically arranged listing of all the forms of a pronoun corresponding to case, number, person, and gender.

Dependent clause: A clause that cannot stand alone as a sentence; it expresses an incomplete thought. Dependent clauses are introduced by words such as *that, who, since, although, because,* etc.

Determiner: A demonstrative or possessive adjective or article that modifies a noun.

> *those* elves   *my* glass   *the* glove

Direct object: The word or phrase that directly receives the action of the verb and that answers the question *What.*

> The dog bit the *man.* (bit what?)

Exclamation point: A mark (!) that indicates sudden emotion; it is placed after the exclamation.

Aha!   What a surprise!

Expletive: A word that adds emphasis or smoothness to a sentence. It fills in where a word is needed.

There are four seasons.

Fragment: A word or group of words that is not a complete sentence. A sentence fragment is usually a word, phrase, or clause that is incorrectly used or placed, thus causing confusion. In the sentence below, *crying* is a fragment since the reader does not know whether it describes *she* or *Fluffy*.

Crying, she held her kitten, Fluffy.

Gender: The classification of words according to the divisions of sex: masculine, feminine, and neuter.

Hyphen: A mark (-) that connects two parts of a word.

de-escalate   ninety-two

Imperative: The mood of a verb that expresses a command or request. The subject of an imperative mood sentence is often *you*, understood.

Stop where you are.   Wake up.

Independent clause: A clause that can stand alone, independently, as a sentence; it expresses a complete thought.

Indicative: The mood of a verb that indicates that the action or condition expressed by the verb is fact.

I am here.   John drives fast.

Indirect object: The word or phrase that indirectly receives the action of the verb and that answers the question *To whom*.

I paid *her* the money. (paid to whom?)

Infinitive: A verbal; a form of a verb using *to*. The infinitive is most often used as a noun, but it can serve as an adjective or adverb as well.

To sculpt was her dream.
I stayed after school *to help*.
They needed permission *to continue*.

Interjection: An expression of strong, sudden emotion or feeling; an exclamation.

Wow!   Yikes!

Linking verb: A verb that connects a subject with a predicate adjective or predicate nominative. The most common linking verb is *be*; other examples include *appear, seem, look*.

I *feel* good.   They *are* runners.

Modify: To change the form by altering, limiting, describing, or qualifying. An adjective modifies a noun by telling more about it.

boat → a small, new, motorized boat

Mood: A form used to express a verb's factuality or the likelihood of the action or condition. The three moods are imperative, indicative, and subjunctive.

Negative: Describing a word, phrase, or sentence that denies, contradicts, or negates. The opposite of affirmative.

No, I won't go.   She is not here.

Nominative: The case of a noun or pronoun that is used as a subject or predicate nominative. This case is also called **subjective**.

They stood.   *It* was *he*.

Noncountable nouns: Nouns that are abstract in quality or quantity; that is, that cannot be totaled, numbered, or counted.

coffee   love   intelligence

Noun: The name of a person, place, thing, idea, quality, activity, etc. Nouns are used as subjects, objects of verbs, objects of prepositions, or appositives.

man, city, screwdriver, democracy, nervousness, game

Noun phrase: A group of words that functions as a noun.

The new clinic is trying to provide a viable *health care delivery system*. I had no choice but *to give them the key*.

Number: The form of a word that indicates whether it is singular or plural.

Object: The word or phrase that identifies the person, place, thing, etc., affected by the predicate in a clause, or that follows and is governed by a preposition.

The man in *uniform* took our *tickets*.

Objective: The case of a noun or pronoun that is used as the object of a verb or preposition.

> The woman in the gray *suit* sold *me this*.

Participle: A verbal; a form of a verb used as an adjective.

> the *spoken* word   a *singing* parrot

> A form of a verb used with an auxiliary verb to indicate certain tenses.

> I have *spoken*.   She is *singing* in her cage.

Passive voice: The verb form that indicates that the subject of the sentence is receiving the action or effect that is expressed by the verb.

> The water was boiled.

Past participle: The principal part of a verb that indicates past or completed action or effect. With an auxiliary, the past participle forms the perfect tenses; alone, it functions as an adjective.

> The book, *written* in only four weeks, has *become* a best seller.

Perfect participle: A form of a verbal consisting of *having* and the past participle.

> *Having abandoned* Plan A, they proceeded to Plan B.

Period: A mark (.) that indicates a completed thought, such as at the end of a sentence or after an abbreviation. Periods used with numbers are called **decimals.**

> Dr.   A.M.   3.1416 $17.98

Person: The form of pronouns that distinguishes among the speaker (*I, we*), the person or item spoken to (*you*), and the person or item spoken about (*he, she, it, they*). These three divisions are called 1st, 2nd, and 3rd person, respectively.

Phrase: A group of related words without a subject or predicate. Phrases must be used in sentences, attached to other words; they cannot stand alone.

> telling a story   around the corner   at 5 o'clock

Plural: The form of nouns, pronouns, and verbs that refers to more than one person or item.

> teeth   children   They play.

Positive: Describing the degree of adjectives and adverbs in which they are simple and not compared.

Also, occasionally, a synonym for affirmative, when speaking of answers, responses, and sentences.

Possessive: The case of a noun or pronoun that indicates ownership or possession. Apostrophes are added to nouns and indefinite pronouns to show possessive case.

Syria's policy   my weapon

Predicate: The word or phrase that expresses the action or being of a subject, or that tells what a subject does. Predicates tell something about subjects. The predicate consists of a verb and any of its auxiliaries or modifiers. Many people use the word synonymously with *verb*.

Predicate adjective: The completion of the thought of a linking verb through description of the subject.

She is *capable*.   This is *painful*.

Predicate nominative: The completion of the thought of a linking verb through identification of the subject.

He is a *spy*.   Those are *sheep*.

Preposition: A word that links a pronoun, noun, or noun phrase with the rest of the sentence, usually describing time, place, or relationship.

of, through, in, with

Present participle: The principal part of a verb that is usually called the progressive form. It indicates continuous or present action. With an auxiliary, it forms the progressive tenses; alone, it functions as an adjective.

They might be *visiting* next week.
The soup *dripping* from your spoon is actually consommé.
Smiling, he opened the door.

Principal parts: The four parts of a verb from which all other forms and uses of a verb can be expressed. The principal parts are present, past, progressive, and past participle. See section 72 for a list of the principal parts of the most commonly used verbs.

Pronoun: A word used in the place of a noun or noun phrase, usually to avoid repetition. Pronouns designate nouns without naming them.

Tamara's relatives thought *they* had more time.

Proper noun: The actual name of a person, place, etc. Proper nouns are always capitalized.

> Paul Bunyan   Mississippi River   IBM

Qualify: To describe, change, restrict, enumerate, or modify a word. An adverb qualifies a verb by telling how often, when, where, how, etc.

Question mark: A mark (?) that indicates an inquiry, interrogation, or direct question. It is placed at the end of a question.

> Where are we?

Quotation marks: Marks (" ") that indicate the beginning and end of someone else's exact spoken or written words.

> She said, "You'll have to go to the end of the line."

Reflexive: Referring to verbs whose objects directly and identically reflect their subjects.

> The child fed herself.

Referring also to pronouns that are direct objects of reflexive verbs. Reflexive pronouns always end with *-self* or *-selves*.

> The children fed themselves.

Relative pronoun: A pronoun that introduces a dependent clause and that refers to some antecedent.

> Stan Lee is the cartoonist *whom* I mentioned.

Semicolon: A mark (;) that indicates a longer pause than a comma but a shorter pause than a period. Semicolons are used between independent clauses that are not joined by coordinate conjunctions and between independent clauses that are joined by conjunctive adverbs.

> Sonia lives in Yuma; her mother lives in Santa Fe.
> We met again today; however, we reached no agreement.

Sentence: A group of related words with a subject and predicate that expresses a complete thought. It begins with a capital letter and ends with a period, question mark, or exclamation point.

Singular: The form of nouns, pronouns, or verbs that refers to only one person or thing.

> tooth   child   He plays.

Subject: The word or phrase in a sentence about which something is said or asserted; it is what the sentence is about. The subject consists of a noun, pronoun, noun phrase, or clause, plus any modifiers. The subject of an imperative mood sentence is understood.

> *The tall, blond man* wore one black shoe.
> Please, sit down. (*You* is the understood subject.)
> *Whether to keep the office open on Saturdays or not* was the question facing the board when it met this afternoon.

Subjunctive: The mood of a verb that expresses hypothetical, contingent, or imaginary action.

> If music *be* the food of love, play on.

Subordinate conjunction: A conjunction that connects a dependent clause with an independent one.

> We'll go *where* we're told.

Superlative: Describing the degree of comparison of adjectives and adverbs that relates three or more items to each other.

> She spoke *the loudest* and *the most distinctly* of all the other actresses on the stage.

Syllable: The smallest separately articulated element of spoken language. Words are divided into syllables to show pronunciation and spelling. A syllable contains one vowel sound and sometimes several consonants.

Tense: A form of a verb that indicates the time of its action or condition.

Verb: A word that states an action, occurrence or being about a noun, pronoun, or noun phrase. The word *verb* is often used as a synonym for *predicate*. A verb may make a statement, ask a question, or give a command.

> go, be, count, seem, prognosticate

Verbal: A word derived from a verb. Verbals are not verbs, but verb forms used as nouns, adjectives, and adverbs. The verbals are gerunds, infinitives, and participles.

Voice: A form of a verb that indicates the relationship between the subject of the verb and the action the verb expresses. The two voices are active and passive.

Vowel: Any of the letters *a, e, i, o,* or *u.*

Review of Grammar and Syntax

Nouns

1. Collective nouns are all singular in form but may be singular or plural in usage. (See also **241**.)

   a. If a collective noun is used so that we think of the entire group (collection), it takes a singular verb.

   > The *committee meets* for its first session next week.
   > My *family* always *goes* on vacation in August.

   Note that the possessive personal pronoun *its* in the first sentence is also singular.

   b. If a collective noun is used so that we think of the members of the group as individuals, it takes a plural verb.

   > The *committee are arguing* among themselves.
   > The *family were brought* to the restaurant one by one.

   Note that the possessive personal pronoun *themselves* in the first sentence is also plural.

2. Quantity nouns, that is, nouns that express some amount, also may be singular or plural. (See also **239**.)

   a. If the quantity is measured as a whole, it takes a singular verb.

   > *Ninety people is* too much for one classroom.
   > *Twelve dollars seems* a fair price for that blouse.

   b. If the quantity is expressed or measured item-by-item or piece-by-piece, it takes a plural verb.

   > *Ninety people are registered* for this course.
   > There *are twelve shirts* in my closet.

   c. When the word *number* is followed by an *of* phrase and is the subject of a sentence (or clause), use this rule:
   If *number* is preceded by *the*, use a singular verb; if it is preceded by any other word, use a plural verb.

   > *The number* of people in the room *is* ninety-three.
   > *A number* of people *have enrolled* in this course.
   > A *large number* of applicants *are* already here.

3. Some nouns are always singular (even though they end in *s* and look plural); thus, they always take singular verbs. Some examples:

athletics	mathematics	physics
civics	mumps	politics
economics	news	statistics
ethics	Philippines	United States

Statistics was my favorite subject in college.
No *news is* good news.
Athletics plays a big part in the daily lives of those students.

4. Some nouns are always plural; thus, they always take plural verbs. Some examples:

belongings	proceeds	tactics
clothes	remains	thanks
goods	riches	trousers
pants	scissors	tweezers
pliers	suds	wages

These *scissors cut* through heavy cardboard.
Tim's *clothes are* on the bed; his *pants*, however, *are* in the closet.
My new *pliers grip* firmly.

Note that the demonstrative pronoun *these* in the first sentence is also plural.

FORMING PLURALS

5. Most nouns form their plurals by adding *s*.

wire	wires	house	houses
pencil	pencils	duck	ducks
Smith	the Smiths	Paula	Paulas

6. Nouns that end in *s, z, ch, sh, tch,* or *x* form their plurals by adding *es*.

tax	taxes	lunch	lunches
glass	glasses	wish	wishes
match	matches	buzz	buzzes
Thomas	the Thomases	Felix	the Felixes

7. Figures, letters, symbols, and any other items that do not have natural plurals form their plurals by adding '*s*.

m	m's	#	#'s
18	18's	+	+'s

8. Nouns that end in *y* form their plurals in one of two ways.

a. If a vowel precedes the *y*, add an *s*.

toy	toys	play	plays
monkey	monkeys	attorney	attorneys

b. If a consonant precedes the *y*, change the *y* to *i* and add *es*.

baby	babies	pharmacy	pharmacies
candy	candies	country	countries

9. Nouns that end in *o* form their plurals in one of two ways.

   a. If a vowel precedes the *o*, or if the noun is a musical term, add an *s*.

cameo	cameos	piano	pianos
alto	altos	radio	radios
ratio	ratios	zoo	zoos

   b. If a consonant precedes the *o*, add *es*.

tomato	tomatoes	torpedo	torpedoes
Negro	Negroes	echo	echoes

10. Hyphenated nouns usually form their plurals by adding *s* to the first word.

mother-in-law	mothers-in-law
editor-in-chief	editors-in-chief

   Note: attorney general   attorneys general

11. Unusual Plurals

   a. Some nouns are the same in both singular and plural forms.

deer	deer	salmon	salmon
fish	fish	sheep	sheep
gross	gross	swine	swine
moose	moose	trout	trout

   b. Some nouns form their plurals according to the rules of the languages from which the noun originated.

alumna	alumnae	datum	data
alumnus	alumni	index	indices
analysis	analyses	medium	media
crisis	crises	radius	radii

   c. Most nouns that end in *f* or *fe* form their plurals by changing their endings to *ves*.

elf	elves	life	lives
half	halves	loaf	loaves
knife	knives	wife	wives
leaf	leaves	wolf	wolves

   Some nouns that end in *f* or *fe*, however, simply add *s*.

belief	beliefs	gulf	gulfs
chief	chiefs	sheriff	sheriffs

d. The plurals of some nouns are completely irregular; thus, they must be memorized.

child	children	mouse	mice
foot	feet	ox	oxen
goose	geese	tooth	teeth
louse	lice	woman	women
man	men		

FORMING POSSESSIVES

12. If a noun is singular, show possession by adding an apostrophe + *s* (*'s*).

attorney	attorney's office	Dolores	Dolores's car
lady	lady's handbag	girl	girl's dog
Tom Clark	Tom Clark's bowling ball	boss	boss's chair

If following this rule makes pronunciation awkward, add only the apostrophe.

Moses	Moses' store	Alexis	Alexis' hair

13. If a noun is plural and it ends in *s*, add an apostrophe after the *s* (*s'*).

attorneys	attorneys' offices	boys	boys' cats
ladies	ladies' handbags	bosses	bosses' chairs
the McCarthys	the McCarthys' cars	girls	girls' dogs

14. If a noun is plural but it doesn't end in *s*, add an apostrophe + *s* (*'s*). (See 11*d* for examples.)

men	men's jackets	women	women's jobs
mice	mice's tails	children	children's voices

15. With a hyphenated noun, show possession by adding *'s* after the last element of the term.

brother-in-law	brother-in-law's house
commander-in-chief	commander-in-chief's desk

16. Compound nouns

   a. Show joint ownership or possession (or ownership by a business firm) by using the apostrophe with the last name only.

   Chan and Tobe*'s* swimming pool (They both own it.)
   Rogers and Hart*'s* musical production (a joint effort)

b. Show separate ownership or possession by using the apostrophe after each name.

> Chan's and Tobe's swimming pools   (Each owns a pool.)
> Rogers' and Hart's homes are separated by a small stone wall.

17. Gerunds that are preceded by a possessive noun require that the noun use an apostrophe.

> Harry's leaving surprised us.
> Jill's swimming has improved rapidly.

18. The possessive form of indefinite pronouns requires an apostrophe. The possessive form of personal pronouns, however, never takes an apostrophe. (See also 21; 34–38.)

one's free time	*My* home is near *yours.*
anybody's guess	*Your* name is the same as *mine.*
somebody else's wallet	This coat is really *hers.*
each other's erasers	*Their* car is old; *ours* is new.
another's children	That must be *somebody else's* hat.
everybody's opinion	It isn't *yours.*

> *Note:* The possessive form of *who* is *whose; who's* is a contraction for *who is* or *who has.*
> The possessive form of *it* is *its; it's* is a contraction for *it is* or *it has.*

19. Use the possessive form of the noun or pronoun even when the noun is understood (not expressed).

> Whose keys did you give me? I gave you *Karen's.* (*Keys* is understood.)
> Kathy's term paper was approved, but *Ed's* (term paper) wasn't.
> You can buy this at Ryan's store or at your own favorite *druggist's* (store).

20. In the case of noun phrases or abbreviations, form the possessive by placing the apostrophe after the last element of the term.

> The U.S.S.R.'s position has not changed.
> Catherine Parr was one of Henry VIII's wives.
> Alexander the Great's journeys took him to India.
> Martha is the boy in the red sweater's mother.
> I paid three month's rent and wished him season's greetings.

EXERCISES
(Answers are on page 51.)

A. Circle the word in parentheses that makes the sentence correct.

1. The team (*plays, play*) its final game next week.

2. The United States (*comprises, comprise*) fifty states.

3. There are three (*Marys, Maries, Mary's*) in my class.

4. The (*bodys, bodies*) of the dead patriots are on display.

5. How many (*mooses, moose*) did you see in the forest?

6. There were six altos and six (*sopranos, sopranoes*) in my sister's choir.

7. What is the (*U.S.A.s, U.S.A.'s*) current policy toward China?

8. The jury (*has, have*) been debating the merits of the case among themselves for hours.

9. Is this your (*sister's-in-law, sister-in-law's*) office?

10. She was looking for the (*womens', women's*) clothing department.

11. Seventy pounds (*is, are*) too much for you to carry.

12. The proceeds from this sale (*goes, go*) to help handicapped children.

13. (*Bettys', Betty's*) stapler broke this afternoon.

14. She chose Kevin's painting, not (*Tims, Tim's*).

15. How many (*sisters-in-law, sister-in-laws*) do you have?

16. Janet has all 32 (*tooths, teeth*) in her mouth.

17. The teacher asked, "Do I have (*everyones, everyone's*) homework?"

18. Their (*secretarie's, secretaries', secretary's*) names are Mr. Kim, Ms. Barber, and Ms. Ginn respectively.

19. After the accident, Leslie had to use (*crutchs, crutches*) for four weeks.

20. How many (*3s, 3's*) are there in your home address?

B. Write the plural form of each of the following nouns in the space provided.

1. David	_____	13. journey	_____
2. court	_____	14. valley	_____
3. office	_____	15. stereo	_____
4. Carter	_____	16. potato	_____
5. mass	_____	17. veto	_____
6. watch	_____	18. father-in-law	_____
7. Jones	_____	19. fish	_____
8. box	_____	20. addendum	_____
9. P	_____	21. hypothesis	_____
10. %	_____	22. half	_____
11. Alex	_____	23. belief	_____
12. county	_____	24. goose	_____

C. Circle the verb in parentheses that makes the sentence correct. (This exercise tests your ability to recognize plural nouns. Remember: If the subject is singular, choose a singular verb [predicate]; if the subject is plural, choose a plural verb [predicate].)

1. (*Is, Are*) 12¢ change all I get from the $5 I gave you?

2. Four paintings (*hangs, hang*) in the living room.

3. What (*is, are*) the number of people in your family?

4. Lyndon Johnson said, "Politics (*is, are*) the art of the possible."

5. My new pliers (*costs, cost*) $3.98.

6. The jury (*has, have*) returned its verdict.

7. A good number of boys in that school (*plays, play*) football.

8. The media (*covers, cover*) all the President's activities.

9. The mothers-in-law (*is, are*) having lunch together.

10. (*Has, Have*) the crisis been resolved to your satisfaction?

11. Mice (*runs, run*) freely throughout the Taylor's barn.

12. At night wolves (*roams, roam*) the countryside.

D. Each of the following sentences contains a possessive noun or pronoun, but the apostrophe or *'s* has been omitted. Show where the apostrophe or the *'s* belongs by rewriting the noun or pronoun in the space provided.

Example: The directors report took three hours to type.   *director's*

1. Last Mondays sales exceeded our expectations.   _____

2. Chris wig was about to fall off, but we caught it.   _____

3. The Petersons driveway always has two cars in it.   _____

4. Our employees salaries usually keep pace with inflation.   _____

5. Gina asked politely where the womens rest room was.   _____

6. If you use your daughter-in-law car, you should arrive before the play begins.   _____

7. Fergusons and Gordons department stores have competed for business for many years.   _____

8. Milly and Al sandwich shop has only been open a year.   _____

9. No one understood the Posts firing of Ms. Plunkett. _____

10. His swimming wasn't nearly as impressive as Jane diving. _____

11. The four friends knew one anothers parents. _____

12. The gown was hers, but the veil was her grandmothers. _____

13. The CPAs office is just down the hall. _____

14. The player of the years jersey hangs in the school's display case. _____

15. Have you read Paul Kinsella *The Techniques of Writing*? _____

ANSWER KEY

The number in parentheses after each answer refers to the rule in this section that covers this point.

A.
1. plays (**1a**)
2. comprises (**3**)
3. Marys (**5**)
4. bodies (**8b**)
5. moose (**11a**)
6. sopranos (**9a**)
7. U.S.A.'s (**20**)
8. have (**1b**)
9. ... law's (**15**)
10. women's (**14**)
11. is (**2a**)
12. go (**4**)
13. Betty's (**12**)
14. Tim's (**19**)
15. sisters ... (**10**)
16. teeth (**11d**)
17. everyone's (**18**)
18. secretaries' (**13**)
19. crutches (**6**)
20. 3's (**7**)

B.
1. Davids (**5**)
2. courts (**5**)
3. offices (**5**)
4. (the) Carters (**5**)
5. masses (**6**)
6. watches (**6**)
7. (the) Joneses (**6**)
8. boxes (**6**)
9. P's (**7**)
10. %'s (**7**)
11. (the) Alexes (**6**)
12. counties (**8b**)
13. journeys (**8a**)
14. valleys (**8a**)
15. stereos (**9a**)
16. potatoes (**9b**)
17. vetoes (**9b**)
18. fathers-in-law (**10**)
19. fish (**11a**)
20. addenda (**11b**)
21. hypotheses (**11b**)
22. halves (**11c**)
23. beliefs (**11c**)
24. geese (**11d**)

C.
1. Is (**2a**)
2. hang (**2b**)
3. is (**2c**)
4. is (**3**)
5. cost (**4**)
6. has (**12**)
7. play (**2c**)
8. cover (**11b**)
9. are (**10**)
10. Has (**11b**)
11. run (**11d**)
12. roam (**11c**)

D.
1. Monday's (**12**)
2. Chris's (**12**)
3. Petersons' (**13**)
4. employees' (**13**)
5. women's (**14**)
6. daughter-in-law's (**15**)
7. Ferguson's and Gordon's (**16b**)
8. Al's (**16a**)
9. Post's (**17**)
10. Jane's (**12; 18**)
11. another's (**18**)
12. grandmother's (**19**)
13. CPA's (**20**)
14. year's (**20**)
15. Kinsella's (**12; 20**)

Pronouns

PERSONAL PRONOUNS

21. Declension of personal pronouns

Case	1st person	2nd person	3rd person
Nominative (subjective)	I, we	you	he, she, it, they
Possessive	my, mine our, ours	your, yours	his, her, hers, its, their, theirs
Objective	me, us	you	him, her, it, them

22. Because of the frequency of errors in personal pronoun usage, note the following:

   a. *You* always takes a plural verb.

   > *You* always *sit* in that same seat, don't you? (one person)
   > *You* always *sit* in those same seats, don't you? (several people)

   b. *He, she,* and *it* are never used with *don't* (the contraction of *do not*); since they are singular, they use the form *doesn't.*

I don't	he doesn't
we don't	she doesn't
you don't	it doesn't
they don't	

   c. Personal pronouns never use an apostrophe to show possession.

   > This is *my* book; it's not *his.*
   > This is *your* book; it's not *hers.*
   > This is *his* book; it's not *mine.*
   > This is *her* book; it's not *yours.*
   > This is *our* book; it's not *theirs.*
   > This is *their* book; it's not *ours.*
   > The cat is licking *its* paws.

   d. *It's* is a contraction of *it is*; *its* is a possessive pronoun.

   > *It's* time for the horse to return to *its* stable.

   e. *Their* is a possessive pronoun; *there* is an expletive.

   > *There* are several maps in *their* classroom.

23. Do not use personal pronouns redundantly, that is, directly after their antecedents.

> *wrong*: Our friends, they went to a museum.
> *right*: Our friends went to a museum.
> *right*: They went to a museum.
>
> *wrong*: My sister, she went to Germany.
> *right*: My sister went to Germany.
> *right*: She went to Germany.

24. In compound constructions, place the personal pronoun last.

> *wrong*: Paul gave the books to me and Joy.
> *right*: Paul gave the books to Joy and me.

The first person pronoun is usually placed last as a mark of courtesy.

> He and I are going to the show together.
> Mother read the paper to him and me.

REFLEXIVE PRONOUNS

25. The only acceptable reflexive forms are:

myself	yourself, yourselves
itself	ourselves
himself	themselves
herself	

26. Reflexive pronouns are compound forms of personal pronouns that are used to refer back to the subject of a sentence; the subject and object are the same.

> The engineer burned *himself*.
> We should give *ourselves* praise for the job we did.
> I hurt *myself* lifting weights today.

Reflexives are also used to give emphasis to someone or something mentioned.

> She *herself* repaired the computer.
> You *yourself* should look up the answer to that question.
> They are going to have to paint this room *themselves*.

27. Reflexives used with *by* mean *alone*.

> I went *by myself*. (I went alone.)
> She repaired the computer *by herself*. (No one helped her.)

28. Reflexives should never be used as the subject of a sentence or as part of a compound subject.

> *wrong*: *Herself* is the cause of the difficulty.
> *right*:   *She* is the cause of the difficulty.

> *wrong*: *Pat and myself* are writing a novel.
> *right*:   *Pat and I* are writing a novel.

29. Reflexives should never be used when an objective case pronoun is called for or as part of a compound object.

> *wrong*: Charles designed the boat *itself*.
> *right*:   Charles designed the boat.
> *right*:   Charles designed *it*.

> *wrong*: Sandra paid Susan and *himself* the money.
> *right*:   Sandra paid Susan and *him* the money.

RELATIVE PRONOUNS

30. Relative pronouns not only refer to antecedents but also introduce dependent clauses. They have specific uses:

Who (*whom* in the objective case) refers only to people.
Whose (the possessive form of *who*) may refer to people or animals.
Which refers to specific animals or things.
That refers to animals, to things, or to people as a class or type.

> Here is the woman *who* will drive your bus.
> The people *whom* you were speaking to were Italians.
> Are these the dogs *whose* kennels you are going to paint?
> Is that the man *whose* house you rented?
> Please look for those papers *which* you filed yesterday.
> Look! There's the cow *which* I milked this morning.
> Rowdy Dancer is the horse *that* won the race.
> The report *that* the President wanted is being prepared now.
> The Native Americans *that* lived in the Plains States were driven out
>   by settlers.

31. Compound forms of relative pronouns are made by adding *-ever* or *-soever*. Such additions add the element of "anyone" or "any way" but do not change the usage of the relative pronoun.

> Please choose *whosoever* raises his or her hand.
> Answer *whichever* way you are directed.

It's going to be expensive, *whichever* one you buy.
We'll vote for *whoever* is nominated.
We'll vote for *whomever* the party nominates.

32. Relative pronouns are singular or plural depending on their antecedents.

> The foreman is reprimanding the *workers who* always *come* late.
>   (*Workers* is plural.)
> *She* is the pilot *who flies* for Eastern Airlines. (*She* is singular.)
> He is one of *those who work* hard.
> He is the *one*, among all others, *who works* the hardest.

DEMONSTRATIVE PRONOUNS

33. Demonstrative pronouns (*this, that, these, those*) refer directly to their nouns. *This* and *that* are singular; *these* and *those* are plural.

> This is my coat.   That is your shoe.
> These are my coats.   Those are your shoes.

34. Note that the nouns *kind, type,* and *sort* are singular. When the demonstrative pronouns are used as adjectives, they must agree with their nouns.

> this kind   that kind   these kinds   those kinds

INDEFINITE PRONOUNS

Indefinite pronouns refer vaguely and indefinitely.

35. The following indefinite pronouns are always singular; thus, they always take singular verbs. (See also 18.)

another	everybody	no one
anybody	everyone	nothing
anyone	everything	one
anything	much	somebody
each	neither	someone
either	nobody	something

it (even if the predicate nominative is plural)

> *Another has taken* your place on the team.
> *Either* of the candidates *seems* qualified.
> *Nothing is* lost and *no one has gained.*
> *Has everyone signed* the guest book?

36. *Every* or *many a* used before a term (or several terms) requires a singular verb.

> *Every* boy and girl on the team *is* a top student.
> *Every* man, woman, and child *was asked* to help row the boat.
> *Many a* worker *looks forward* to the weekend.
> *Many a* graduate fondly *remembers* the old school days.

37. The following indefinite pronouns are always plural; thus, they always take plural verbs:

> both   few   many   others   several

> *Many are called* but *few are chosen.*
> *Others have tried* this lock but no one has succeeded.

38. Some indefinite pronouns are singular or plural, depending on their meanings.

> all   any   more   most   none   some

> *Is* there *any* who will speak for him?
> *Are any* of them here today?
> *Most* of what you say *is* true.
> *Most* of the students usually *arrive* on time.

39. Use the indefinite pronoun *one* to mean *anyone, everyone,* or *someone.*

> When *someone* is happy, the world seems bright.
> When *one* is happy, the world seems bright.

Use the personal pronoun *you* only when addressing a specific person or persons. Use the indefinite pronoun *one* when addressing people in general.

> *poor*:   You should take care of your body. (unless addressing a particular person)
> *better*: *One* should take care of one's body.

40. Use *some, someone, somebody, something* in affirmative statements and in questions. (See also 140.)

> There's *somebody* else in this room; I can feel it.
> I need *some.*
> I have *some* rare coins.
> Won't you have *some* pie?

Use *any, anyone, anybody, anything* in negative statements and in questions.

> I don't have *any* rare coins in my pocket.
> Do you have *any* rare coins in your pocket?

Is there *anybody* else in this room?
No, there isn't *anybody* else here.
Do you have *any*? No, I don't have *any*.

PRONOUNS AND CASE

41. Nominative (or subjective) case pronouns (*I, you, he, she, it, we, they, who*) are used in two instances:

    a. When the pronoun is the subject of a sentence.

    > Heather and *I* want to live in the mountains.
    > *You* and Tara want to live in the city.
    > *It* rains in June in Mexico City.
    > *He* and *she* are traveling in Europe now.
    > *We* already have that medical journal.
    > *They*'ll take care of your plants while you're gone.
    > *Who* asked you for Elaine's address?

    b. In the predicative nominative, that is, after linking verbs. With pronouns, the most commonly used linking verb is *to be* (*am, are, is, were, was, be, being, been*).

    > Who is at the door? It *is I.*
    > I am sure that it *was she* whom you saw.
    > *Was* it *he* who asked for directions to the White House?
    > When we answer the phone, I'm sure that it *will be they.*

42. Possessive case pronouns (*my, mine, your, yours, his, her, hers, its, our, ours, their, theirs, whose*) are used to show ownership or possession. These words never take an apostrophe. (See also **18** and **22c**.)

    > This typewriter isn't *mine*; it's *yours.*
    > *Her* ribbon wasn't *hers* after she sold it.
    > *They* fully deserved to win; the victory was *theirs.*

    Use a possessive case pronoun with a gerund when appropriate.

    > *Her leaving* was more surprising than *his staying.*

43. Objective case pronouns (*me, you, him, her, it, us, them, whom*) are used in three instances:

    a. When the pronoun is the direct object of a verb. In these examples, the pronouns are receiving the action of the verbs *asked, would invite, did invite,* and *will ask.*

    > She asked *me.*
    > I wondered if she would invite *him.*
    > *Whom* did you invite?
    > Will Paul ask *them* and *us* to collect tickets tonight?

b. When the pronoun is the indirect object of a verb.
In these examples, the pronouns are receiving the action of the verbs indirectly. The direct objects in these examples are *form, order, stereo,* and *question.*

> Ms. Roberts gave *us* the application form.
> Phyllis sent *them* the order that they had requested.
> Bert sold *her* the most expensive stereo in the shop.
> I turned on the computer and asked *it* the hardest question I could think of.

c. When the pronoun is the object of a preposition.
In these examples, the pronouns are objects of the prepositions *for, by, to, between,* and *with.*

> Will you please hold Jim's screwdriver for *him?*
> The letter was written by *her.*
> *Whom* were you talking to in the cafeteria?
> Between *you* and *me,* I don't think the new plan will work.
> Bob asked Mary to go swimming with Polly and *me.*

44. When a pronoun is used with an appositive, determine the case of the pronoun by ignoring the appositive.

> We boys are having a good time here at camp.
> (We are having a good time at camp.)

> Was that criticism directed at us girls?
> (Was that criticism directed at us?)

45. *than, as,* and *like* (See also **181.**)

a. *Than* is a conjunction that is used in a comparison to introduce the second element. When that element is implied or understood, the case of the pronoun should be the same as the case of the noun or pronoun in the first element. Mentally adding a word or two can help you decide which is the correct case to use.

> She is a much better student than *he.* (is)
> He drives more quickly than *I.* (drive)
> I am taller than *you.* (are tall)
> They would rather eat with Archie than (with) *me.*
> Peg likes me better than (she likes) *him.*

b. *As* is also a conjunction used in comparisons.

> Her sister is not as tall as *she.* (is tall)
> Bill's brother was not so smart as *he.* (was smart)
> Do you like her as much as *I?* (like her)
> Do you like her as much as (you like) *me?*

c. *Like* can be a verb or preposition. When *like* is a preposition and is followed by a pronoun, that pronoun must be in the objective case.

It's not *like her* to run from responsibility.
My brother always wanted me to act *like him.*
Sheila looks *like me*, doesn't she?

PRONOUNS AND THEIR ANTECEDENTS

46. The relationship between a pronoun and the noun to which it refers—its antecedent—must be clear. If pronouns are vague, unclear, or carelessly used, the sentence should be rewritten.

poor: Rachel told Sara that she should take some vitamins.
better: Rachel said to Sara, "Take some vitamins."

poor: Elizabeth read that in Belgium they eat a lot of potatoes.
better: Elizabeth read that Belgians eat a lot of potatoes.

poor: We'll take the plane up for a test flight today, if the weather is good, which I think it is.
better: We'll take the plane up for a test flight today, if the weather is as good as I think it is.

47. Pronouns must agree with their antecedents in case, in gender, and in number. The following are examples of agreement in gender and number.

The *girl* ate *her* meal. (feminine, singular)
The *boy* ate *his* meal. (masculine, singular)
The *cat* ate *its* meal. (neuter, singular)
They all ate *their* meals together. (plural)
We ate *our* meals together. (plural)

48. Since collective nouns can be singular or plural, depending on their usage, the pronouns referring to them must reflect the intended meaning. (See also **1a; 1b.**)

The *team* lost *its* sixth game in a row. (singular meaning)
The *team* complained about *their* loose jerseys. (plural meaning)

The *committee* meets for *its* final session next week. (singular meaning)
The *committee* are arguing among *themselves*. (plural meaning)

49. When indefinite pronouns are used as antecedents, their pronouns must agree in number.

    a. The following are singular indefinite pronouns; when used as antecedents, they require singular pronouns. (See also 35.)

another	either	much	one
anybody	everybody	neither	somebody
anyone	everyone	nobody	someone
anything	everything	no one	something
each	it	nothing	

    The school will accept *anyone* if *he/she* seems worthy.
    Each of us knows *his/her* social security number.
    Neither of our products is selling at *its* best.

    b. The following are plural indefinite pronouns; when used as antecedents, they require plural pronouns.

    both   few   many   others   several

    Many enjoy *their* vacations in Rehoboth.
    Both of the applicants are worthy, at least on *their* résumés.
    Few can remember when *they* were two years old.

    c. The following indefinite pronouns may be singular or plural, depending on their usage; when used as antecedents, one must determine the meaning of the sentence.

    all   any   more   most   none   some

    Is there *any who* will speak for him? (singular)
    Are *any* of *them* here today? (plural)
    All in the crowd cheered *their* approval. (plural)
    All the money is in *its* proper place. (singular)

50. Ignore prepositional phrases, appositives, asides, and explanatory phrases when determining the true antecedent in a sentence.

    Beth, along with the two others, studied *her* piano lesson.
    Roland, and not his nephews, is on *his* way here now.
    Each of our nearest neighbors has a van in *his* driveway.
    Ed, our regional director of Midwest sales, has *his* office in Des Moines.
    Washington's *monuments*, as well as the Museum of American History, have scheduled *their* hours later this summer.

51. When two or more antecedents are joined by *and*, the pronoun is plural.

    Mae and Tillie have just mowed *their* front lawn.
    The *boys and girls* asked us to repeat what we'd said to *them*.

52. *or/nor* joining antecedents:

    a. When the antecedent closest to the verb is singular, the pronoun is also singular.

        Neither Tillie *nor Mae* has just mowed *her* lawn.
        Either Barry *or* his *sister* will get *her* wish.

    b. When the antecedent closest to the verb is plural, the pronoun is also plural.

        Neither Mae *nor* Tillie's *children* have just mowed *their* lawn.
        Either Barry *or* his *sisters* will get *their* wish.

53. *Who/whom* may refer to a singular or plural antecedent. In determining the case of the pronoun (*who* is nominative, *whom* is objective), look only to its own clause, not to the clause of the antecedent.

    Reverend Malloy was the pastor *whom* we all admired.
    (*Whom* refers to the singular, nominative case noun *Reverend Malloy*, but in its own clause *whom* is the object of the verb *admired*; thus, it is objective case.)

    We loved the family *who* lived next door.
    (*Who* refers to the plural, objective case noun *family*, but in its own clause *who* is the subject of the verb *lived*; thus, it is nominative case.)

EXERCISES
(Answers are on page 67.)

A. Circle the word in parentheses that makes the sentence correct.

    1. Peter and (*I, myself*) planned the picnic for the club.

    2. Have most of the members cast (*his/her, their*) votes yet?

    3. Ethel applied for the new position, but then decided that it wasn't for (*she, her*).

    4. This isn't Julie's, and it isn't (*hers, her's*) either.

    5. Mom told (*me and Lynn, Lynn and me*) to get the mail.

    6. Do you have (*something, anything*) for a headache?

    7. (*Which, Whichever*) one you choose, I'm sure you'll enjoy it.

8. I suggest that everyone bring (*his/her, their*) passport to the testing office.

9. (*Has, Have*) everybody brought an umbrella today?

10. Howard used to say, "Tell it (*like, as*) it is."

11. Neither Frances nor her two friends were chosen to hang (*her, their*) paintings in the exhibit.

12. Every girl in this scout troop (*is, are*) being asked to participate in the cookie sale.

13. Do we know if (*its, it's*) acceptable to wear jeans to the party?

14. This is the man (*who, that*) will fix your sink.

15. (*This, These*) kind of party is always fun, don't you think?

16. Did she say that (*we, us*) runners could compete?

17. You (*youself, yourself*) should be able to figure out the answer to this math problem.

18. As soon as the door opened, I knew that it would be (*she, her*).

19. My father always thought that I looked like (*he, him*).

20. The church, as well as all the surrounding buildings, has had (*its, their*) water supply cut.

21. How much money is (*there, their*) in the cash box?

B. Each of the following sentences contains one pronoun that is incorrect. Cross out the incorrect pronoun and write the correct pronoun in the space provided.

Example: Jim doesn't always wear ~~her~~ seat belt.   _____*his*_____

1. They weighed theirselves on the store scale.   _____

2. Yourself should be held responsible for this act.   _____

3. Patti gave the keys to Lauri and myself. _____

4. Are you the plumber which I called to stop the leak? _____

5. Who's notebook is on the floor? _____

6. She is the kind of worker which we look for. _____

7. You may pick which dessert you like best from this tray. _____

8. This sorts of actions are intolerable at Wimbledon. _____

9. The book advised us all, "You should try to get eight hours of sleep at night." _____

10. Aren't there some eggs in the refrigerator? _____

11. Whom said, "The fewer our wants, the more we resemble the gods"? _____

12. I can't believe that she won; it should have been him. _____

13. If it isn't her's, then whose is it? _____

14. Tony asked Joan to go to the beach with Dennis and I. _____

15. Us kids never get to stay up past midnight. _____

16. Donna is a much faster worker than me. _____

17. The jury turned in their verdict to the bailiff. _____

18. Everyone knows where their children are. _____

19. Several in the room remembered his experiences at summer camp. _____

20. The House and Senate adjourned its deliberation early this spring. _____

C. First review the nominative and objective pronoun cases in the list below. Then circle the pronoun in parentheses that makes the sentence correct.

| Nominative: | I | you | he | she | it | we | they | who |
| Objective: | me | you | him | her | it | us | them | whom |

1. (*Who, Whom*) did you say came to visit while I was gone?

2. The speaker (*who, whom*) we expected never showed up.

3. When I asked who was knocking on the door, my uncle answered, "It is (*I, me*)."

4. They weren't sure that (*we, us*) could climb the hill.

5. I told (*they, them*) not to come in until they'd wiped their feet.

6. Melanie hired her sister and (*I, me*) for the job.

7. The boys divided the pizza among (*they, them*).

8. Jackie is going to share her room with you and (*I, me*), isn't she?

9. I hope to be able to give (*he and she, him and her*) as much time to finish as they need.

10. Let's measure to see if we are taller than (*they, them*).

11. I'll bet that they're not as tall as (*we, us*).

12. (*Her and I, She and I, She and me*) were tied for first place in the spelling contest.

D. Circle the verb in parentheses that makes the sentence correct. (This exercise tests your ability to make the verb agree in number with the pronoun subject.)

1. I'm pretty sure that he (*doesn't, don't*) know her.

2. I know several people who (*knows, know*) how to tune up a Volkswagen.

3. Neither of the animals (*has, have*) been house trained.

4. It (*is, are*) four new tires that you'll have to buy, not two.

5. Every one of them (*looks, look*) good enough to eat.

6. Many a law student (*crams, cram*) for exams.

7. (*Is, Are*) there a few of you veterans in the audience?

8. (*Is, Are*) there more of those cookies left?

9. (*Is, Are*) there more of that pie left?

10. I, as well as my parents, my grandparents, and my brother, (*feels, feel*) that our city is the best in the whole state.

11. We, the proprietors of this restaurant, (*promises, promise*) to keep prices low.

12. Both of us (*believe, believes*) that you need a math tutor this summer.

E. Identify the antecedent and the pronoun that refers to it in each of the following sentences. Indicate whether the pronoun is singular (*S*) or plural (*P*).

	antecedent	pronoun	number
Example: Ann is fond of her cat.	*Ann*	*her*	*S*
1. The Senate voted itself a raise in pay.			
2. They painted that room by themselves.			
3. Was it I to whom you just spoke?			
4. Are you sure this is the painting which you commissioned?			
5. I am the only one of the people here who knows the secret.			
6. He is one of the men who works here.			
7. Our team is proud of its victory.			

	antecedent	pronoun	number

8. Either Ms. Talamini or her boys have just arrived in their car.

   _____   _____   _____

9. Many can recall their wedding days vividly.

   _____   _____   _____

10. None of the cheerleaders re-membered their new shoes.

   _____   _____   _____

11. None of the bread has been taken from its package.

   _____   _____   _____

12. Mr. Essig, as well as Mr. Moreno, is on his way to the meeting.

   _____   _____   _____

13. Not only Susan, but also Charles, will wash his car.

   _____   _____   _____

14. Kurt is a driver whom we can rely on.

   _____   _____   _____

ANSWER KEY

A.
1. I (24; 48)
2. their (49*c*)
3. her (43*c*)
4. hers (22*c*; 42)
5. Lynn and me (24)
6. anything (40)
7. Whichever (31)
8. his/her (49*a*)
9. Has (35)
10. as (45*b*)
11. their (52*b*)
12. is (36)
13. it's (22*d*)
14. who (30)
15. This (24)
16. we (44)
17. yourself (25)
18. she (41*b*)
19. him (45*c*)
20. its (50)
21. there (22*e*)

B.

	Incorrect	Correct		Incorrect	Correct
1.	theirselves	themselves (25)	11.	Whom	Who (41*a*)
2.	Yourself	You (28)	12.	him	he (41*b*)
3.	myself	me (29)	13.	her's	hers (42)
4.	which	whom (30; 53)	14.	I	me (43*c*)
5.	Who's	Whose (30)	15.	Us	We (44)
6.	which	that (30)	16.	me	I (45*a*)
7.	which	whichever (31)	17.	their	its (48)
8.	This	These, Those (34)	18.	their	his/her (49*a*)
9.	You	One (39)	19.	his	their (49*b*)
10.	some	any (40)	20.	its	their (51)

C.
1. Who (53)
2. whom (53)
3. I (41*b*)
4. we (41*a*)
5. them (43*b*)
6. me (43*a*)
7. them (43*c*)
8. me (43*c*)
9. him and her (43*b*)
10. they (45*a*)
11. we (45*b*)
12. She and I (24; 41*a*)

D.
1. doesn't (22*b*)
2. know (32)
3. has (35)
4. is (35)
5. looks (35)
6. crams (36)
7. Are (37)
8. Are (38)
9. Is (38)
10. feel (50)
11. promise (50)
12. believe (37)

E.

	antecedent	pronoun	number		antecedent	pronoun	number
1.	Senate	itself	S (26)	8.	boys	their	P (52*b*)
2.	They	themselves	P (27)	9.	Many	their	P (49*b*)
3.	I	whom	S (30)	10.	None	their	P (49*c*)
4.	painting	which	S (30)	11.	None	its	S (49*c*)
5.	one	who	S (32)	12.	Mr. Essig	his	S (50)
6.	men	who	P (32)	13.	Charles	his	S (52*a*)
7.	team	its	S (48)	14.	Kurt	whom	S (53)

Verbs

TYPES OF VERBS

The three types of verbs are transitive, intransitive, and linking verbs.

54. Transitive verbs take direct objects to complete their meanings. Some verbs that are always transitive are *bring* and *carry*. One has to bring something or carry something or someone.

    > The hen laid an egg.
    > Postal clerks mailed our packages.
    > I raised the window.

    Egg, packages, and *window* are all receivers of actions; they are direct objects.

55. Intransitive verbs do not take direct objects. The action of the verbs is not carried on to objects; it is complete in itself. Most verbs can be used without objects, at least in their progressive forms; some verbs are always intransitive, such as *arrive, complain, disagree, fall, grumble, look, succeed, swim,* and *travel.*

    > My uncle lay down for a nap.
    > She rose from her nap at five o'clock.
    > Please, sit down!

    To see if a verb is transitive or intransitive, ask the question *Who?* or *What?* If either question cannot be answered of the verb, then it is intransitive. In the examples, notice that one cannot answer the questions *My uncle lay what?* or *She rose what?* or *Sit what?* In contrast, notice that one can answer the questions in item 54: *The hen laid what?, Postal clerks mailed what?, I raised what?*

56. Linking (or copulative or state-of-being) verbs are not action verbs. They may take predicate nouns (predicate nominatives) or predicate adjectives, but never adverbs.

    a. Linking verbs may be any part of the verb *be.*

    > She *is* an actress.
    > That plant *will be* healthy after we add fertilizer.
    > Dave *could have been* a nurse, but he changed his mind.

    b. Linking verbs may also be sensing verbs, such as *feel, look, smell, sound,* and *taste*; these verbs are followed by a predicate adjective.

    > He *feels* good today.
    > She *looks* beautiful.

This *smells* great, but it *tastes* funny.
Your voice *sounds* hoarse.

c. Linking verbs may also be appearance verbs, such as *appear, become, grow, prove, remain,* and *seem,* when the meaning is *is* or some part of *be.*

My grandfather *remains* sick. (He is still sick.)
He *seems* bright. (To me he is bright.)
Your tomatoes *are growing* strong, but they *appear* spindly. (They are strong, but they are also weak-looking.)

MOOD

The mood of verbs (indicative, imperative, subjective) is the manner in which actions are expressed.

57. The *indicative mood* is factual. It states a fact or asks a question either positively or negatively. It is the most common mood.

I mailed some letters.
Did you mail any postcards?
No, I didn't mail any postcards.

58. The *imperative mood* is used for commands and wishes. It is used only in the present tense.

Leave here immediately!
Please go.
Make a U-turn and then turn left.

The subject *you,* whether singular or plural, is understood, that is, not expressed. The negative form of the imperative mood uses *don't.*

Don't go near the water.
Don't leave the window open.

59. Sometimes a sentence that looks like an indicative mood question will actually have an imperative mood meaning.

Will you get that light as you leave.
(This actually means "Please turn off the light.")
Do you want to come with me.
(When this is said by a receptionist who is ushering you into your doctor's office, it actually means "Follow me, please.")

Because these sentences are not truly questions (the receptionist really doesn't want you to answer "Yes, I do" or "No, I don't"), they do not conclude with question marks. Notice that both examples end with periods.

60. Most grammarians believe that the *subjunctive mood* is on its way out, that is, outmoded and used by fewer and fewer people every year. They're probably correct, but for now—for purposes of passing the TOEFL—learn these dated ways of using this mood.

The subjunctive mood is used for orders, suppositions, contrary-to-fact conditions, future possibilities, doubts, wishes, and necessities. The most common of these are conditions contrary to actual fact, and wishes. The main idea of the subjunctive mood is the expression of a hypothetical or contingent event.

If Rosa were at this concert, it would be more fun. (contrary to fact)
I wish they were strong enough to help us. (wish)
She acts as if she were richer than he. (doubt)
If it be true, let us proceed. (future possibility)
If "if's" were horses, beggars would ride. (supposition)

61. Note that in most subjunctive mood sentences the situations are known to be untrue. In the first example in section **60**, we know that Rosa is not at the concert. On the other hand, if we did not know for certain that she would be at the concert, then the sentence might be in the indicative mood.

If Rosa is at this concert, I surely don't see her.
(We do not know for certain that Rosa is not here.)

62. The subjunctive mood of most verbs is different from the indicative mood only in the third person singular. In the subjunctive, the *s* is dropped from the third person singular verb.

indicative: He exercises every day.
subjunctive: It is important that he exercise every day.
indicative: I'm sure that Mrs. Kowalski was speaking from experience.
subjunctive: I wish Mrs. Kowalski were speaking from experience.

63. The subjunctive mood of the verb *be* uses *be* throughout the present tense and *were* throughout the past tense. The verb *be* is the most commonly used verb in the subjunctive mood.

It is important that you *be* on your guard.
I wish I *were* as graceful as my sister.
We wish we *were* able to attend your graduation ceremonies.
If music *be* the food of love, play on.

64. Subjunctive mood sentences that are conditional—and most of them are —have two clauses, one main or independent and one dependent. The dependent clause begins with *if*. Note well the following tense progressions in this type of construction:

a. *future-possible*

When the *if*-conditional sentence has the dependent clause in the present tense, the main clause is in the future tense. This is called a *future-possible* condition.

> If you hurry, you'll be there on time.
> If I follow the directions carefully, this cake will be delicious.
> If I write faster, I'll finish on time.

b. *present-unreal*

When the *if*-conditional sentence has the dependent clause in the past tense, the main clause uses *would, should, could,* or *might.* This is called a *present-real* condition.

> If you hurried, you'd be there on time.
> If I followed the directions carefully, this cake would be delicious.
> If I had the time, I'd take a vacation.
> If she were here, she could show you.
> I might finish on time if I wrote faster.

c. *past-unreal*

When the *if*-conditional sentence has the dependent clause in the past perfect tense, the main clause uses *would have, should have, could have,* or *might have.* This is called a *past-unreal* condition.

> If I had hurried, I'd have been on time.
> If I had followed the directions carefully, this cake would have been delicious.
> If I had had the time, I'd have taken a vacation.
> If she had been here, she could have shown you.
> I might have finished on time if I had written faster.

65. When using the subjunctive mood to express a wish (suggesting a contrary-to-fact condition), use the past tense to suggest present action; use the past perfect tense to suggest past action.

> I wish she were here now to show us. (present action)
> I wish she had been here yesterday. (past action)
> She wishes she had written more often. (past action)
> I wish I were capable of resolving the situation. (present action)

66. When a subjunctive mood dependent clause is introduced by *until, when, before, as soon as, unless, as long as,* or *while,* the clause takes the present tense to describe the future.

> We won't go unless they invite us.
> They will stay as long as we are here.
> I'll ride until they call me in for dinner.
> You won't learn while you keep your eyes closed.

67. The subjunctive mood is often still used with clauses that begin with *that* following *demand, insist, recommend, require, suggest,* and the phrase *it is necessary.*

> The headmaster demanded that the boys be in line by 8 o'clock.
> Her gardener recommended that she plant cherry tomatoes. He also suggested that she water them daily.

68. The mood of a sentence should always be consistent, that is, it should not shift needlessly.

> *wrong*: If I were you and was lost, I'd ask directions.
> *right*: If I were you and were lost, I'd ask directions.

> *wrong*: If I had had the training and had the motivation, I'd have become an engineer.
> *right*: If I had had the training and had had the motivation, I'd have become an engineer.
> *right*: If I had had the training and the motivation, I'd have become an engineer.

VOICE

The voice of verbs (active and passive) indicates the relationships between the subjects and the actions expressed by their verbs.

69. The active voice shows that the subject of the sentence is the actor or doer of the action.

> Irene *bought* a cutting board.
> We *hear* noises in all parts of our house.
> They*'ll open* their doors next month.

70. The passive voice shows that the subject of the sentence is being acted upon, that is, is receiving the action of the verb. The passive voice is formed by using some part of the verb *be* plus the past participle of the main verb. It is used to draw attention or give emphasis to the receiver of the action or to state generalizations. It is also used to keep a distance, that is, to maintain an impersonal position.

> The cutting board *was bought* by Irene.
> Noises *are heard* in all parts of our house.
> Their doors *will be opened* next month.

The passive voice may also be used to perform the function of a linking verb.

> Martin Luther King *was considered* a spiritual leader.
> Abe Lincoln *has been called* The Great Emancipator.

71. The voice of verbs should always be consistent, that is, it should not shift needlessly.

> *wrong*: He gave me my pay and I was told where to go.
> *right*: He gave me my pay and told me where to go.

> *wrong*: We reclosed the box after its contents had been carefully examined.
> *right*: We reclosed the box after we had carefully examined its contents.

TENSE

Tense means "time." The tense of a verb indicates and establishes time and its relationship to events in a sentence.

72. Principal parts of a verb

It is necessary to know the principal parts of a verb in order to know how to form the various tenses. For regular verbs, the present is the same as the infinitive (*talk, to talk*); the past is made by adding *d* or *ed* to the present (*talked*); the present participle (also called the progressive or continuous) is made by adding *ing* to the present (*talking*); the past participle is the same as the past but is preceded by *have* or *has* (*I have talked; he has talked*).

There are many irregular verbs, however, that form their principal parts in an irregular manner. Following is a selected list of irregular verbs and their principal parts. Knowing the parts, one can form all the simple and perfect tenses. The list is long but important. Memorizing it in short sections will make the task easier. What are the patterns in some of the groupings?

Present	Past	Progressive	Past Participle (with *have* or *has*)
become	became	becoming	become
come	came	coming	come
cost	cost	costing	cost
cut	cut	cutting	cut
do	did	doing	done
get	got	getting	got, gotten
go	went	going	gone
have	had	having	had
hear	heard	hearing	heard
hold	held	holding	held
lay	laid	laying	laid
lead	led	leading	led
let	let	letting	let
lie (recline)	lay	lying	lain

Present	Past	Progressive	Past Participle (with *have* or *has*)
lie (tell an untruth)	lied	lying	lied
make	made	making	made
meet	met	meeting	met
put	put	putting	put
quit	quit	quitting	quit
say	said	saying	said
show	showed	showing	shown
tear	tore	tearing	torn
wear	wore	wearing	worn
win	won	winning	won
arise	arose	arising	arisen
eat	ate	eating	eaten
fall	fell	falling	fallen
forbid	forbade	forbidding	forbidden
give	gave	giving	given
take	took	taking	taken
write	wrote	writing	written
break	broke	breaking	broken
choose	chose	choosing	chosen
forget	forgot	forgetting	forgotten
speak	spoke	speaking	spoken
steal	stole	stealing	stolen
feel	felt	feeling	felt
keep	kept	keeping	kept
leave	left	leaving	left
lend	lent	lending	lent
lose	lost	losing	lost
mean	meant	meaning	meant
sleep	slept	sleeping	slept
spend	spent	spending	spent
sweep	swept	sweeping	swept
weep	wept	weeping	wept
begin	began	beginning	begun
drink	drank	drinking	drunk
ring	rang	ringing	rung
run	ran	running	run
sing	sang	singing	sung
swim	swam	swimming	swum
fly	flew	flying	flown
grow	grew	growing	grown

Present	Past	Progressive	Past Participle (with *have* or *has*)
know	knew	knowing	known
throw	threw	throwing	thrown
bring	brought	bringing	brought
buy	bought	buying	bought
fight	fought	fighting	fought
teach	taught	teaching	taught
think	thought	thinking	thought

73. Complete conjugation of two verbs, *to see* and *to be*
Principal parts of *to see*: see, saw, seeing, seen

Indicative Mood

ACTIVE VOICE

PERSON	SINGULAR	PLURAL

Present Tense

1	I see	we see
2	you see	you see
3	he, she, it sees	they see

Past Tense

1	I saw	we saw
2	you saw	you saw
3	he, she, it saw	they saw

Future Tense

1	I shall, will see	we shall, will see
2	you will see	you will see
3	he, she, it will see	they will see

Present Perfect Tense

1	I have seen	we have seen
2	you have seen	you have seen
3	he, she, it has seen	they have seen

Past Perfect Tense

1	I had seen	we had seen
2	you had seen	you had seen
3	he, she, it had seen	they had seen

PERSON	SINGULAR	PLURAL

Future Perfect Tense

1	I shall, will have seen	we shall, will have seen
2	you will have seen	you will have seen
3	he, she, it will have seen	they will have seen

Present Progressive Tense

1	I am seeing	we are seeing
2	you are seeing	you are seeing
3	he, she, it is seeing	they are seeing

Past Progressive Tense

1	I was seeing	we were seeing
2	you were seeing	you were seeing
3	he, she, it was seeing	they were seeing

Future Progressive Tense

1	I shall, will be seeing	we shall, will be seeing
2	you will be seeing	you will be seeing
3	he, she, it will be seeing	they will be seeing

Present Perfect Progressive Tense

1	I have been seeing	we have been seeing
2	you have seen seeing	you have been seeing
3	he, she, it has been seeing	they have been seeing

Past Perfect Progressive Tense

1	I had been seeing	we had been seeing
2	you had been seeing	you had been seeing
3	he, she, it had been seeing	they had been seeing

Future Perfect Progressive Tense

1	I shall, will have been seeing	we shall, will have been seeing
2	you will have been seeing	you will have been seeing
3	he, she, it will have been seeing	they will have been seeing

Indicative Mood

PASSIVE VOICE

PERSON	SINGULAR	PLURAL

Present Tense

1	I am seen	we are seen
2	you are seen	you are seen
3	he, she, it is seen	they are seen

Past Tense

1	I was seen	we were seen
2	you were seen	you were seen
3	he, she, it was seen	they were seen

Future Tense

1	I shall, will be seen	we shall, will be seen
2	you will be seen	you will be seen
3	he, she, it will be seen	they will be seen

Present Perfect Tense

1	I have been seen	we have been seen
2	you have been seen	you have been seen
3	he, she, it has been seen	they have been seen

Past Perfect Tense

1	I had been seen	we had been seen
2	you had been seen	you had been seen
3	he, she, it had been seen	they had been seen

Future Perfect Tense

1	I shall, will have been seen	we shall, will have been seen
2	you will have been seen	you will have been seen
3	he, she, it will have been seen	they will have been seen

Present Progressive Tense

1	I am being seen	we are being seen
2	you are being seen	you are being seen
3	he, she, it is being seen	they are being seen

Past Progressive Tense

1	I was being seen	we were being seen
2	you were being seen	you were being seen
3	he, she, it was being seen	they were being seen

The future progressive, present perfect progressive, past perfect progressive, and future perfect progressive tenses are not used in the passive voice.

Subjunctive Mood

ACTIVE VOICE

Present Tense: (if) I, you, he, she, it, we, you, they see
Past Tense: (if) I, you, he, she, it, we, you, they saw

Subjunctive Mood

PASSIVE VOICE

Present Tense: (if) I, you, he, she, it, we, you, they be seen
Past Tense: (if) I, you, he, she, it, we, you, they were seen

Imperative Mood

Active Voice: (you) see   *Passive Voice*: (you) be seen

Verbals

ACTIVE VOICE

Present Infinitive: to see
Perfect Infinitive: to have seen
Present Gerund: seeing
Perfect Gerund: having seen
Present Participle: seeing
Past Participle: seen
Perfect Participle: having seen

PASSIVE VOICE

Present Infinitive: to be seen
Perfect Infinitive: to have been seen
Present Gerund: being seen
Perfect Gerund: having been seen
Present Participle: being seen
Perfect Participle: having been seen

The verb *be* does not use the passive voice or the progressive tenses.
Principal parts of *to be*: be, was, being, been

Indicative Mood

ACTIVE VOICE

PERSON	SINGULAR	PLURAL

Present Tense

1	I am	we are
2	you are	you are
3	he, she, it is	they are

Past Tense

1	I was	we were
2	you were	you were
3	he, she, it was	they were

Future Tense

1	I shall, will be	we shall, will be
2	you will be	you will be
3	he, she, it will be	they will be

Present Perfect Tense

1	I have been	we have been
2	you have been	you have been
3	he, she, it has been	they have been

Past Perfect Tense

1	I had been	we had been
2	you had been	you had been
3	he, she, it had been	they had been

PERSON	SINGULAR	PLURAL

Future Perfect Tense

1	I shall, will have been	we shall, will have been
2	you will have been	you will have been
3	he, she, it will have been	they will have been

Subjunctive Mood

Present Tense: (if) I, you, he, she, it, we, you, they be
Past Tense: (if) I, you, he, she, it, we, you, they were
Future Tense: (if) I, you, he, she, it, we, you, they should be
Present Perfect Tense: (if) I, you, he, she, it, we, you, they have been
Past Perfect Tense: (if) I, you, he, she, it, we, you, they had been

There is only one form of the imperative mood for the verb *be*: be

Simple Tenses: present, past, and future

74. The present tense is used to express one of four conditions:

a. present time or continued, habitual action

I *hear* you.　　We *need* food.

b. general truth

The earth *revolves* around the sun and *rotates* on its axis.

c. historical present

Jefferson *ranks* as one of our great presidents.

d. the future

We *leave* for Miami on Tuesday; our plane *arrives* at 9:05.

Remember that the 3rd person singular of the present tense (*he, she, it*) requires an *s*.

Do and *does* are used as auxiliary verbs in the present tense either to emphasize the action of the verb or to ask questions.

I do hear you. (as though someone thought you didn't hear)
The earth does revolve around the sun. (as though someone wasn't certain and needed to be convinced)
Does Jefferson rank as one of our great presidents?
Do we leave for Miami on Tuesday?

75. The past tense is used to express an activity that ended sometime in the past.

> I *got up* this morning and *ate* breakfast.
> They *went* home at 4:15.

76. The future tense describes actions that have not yet happened.

a. One way to express the future is to use *shall* or *will* + the simple form of the verb. *Shall* and *will* are often contracted when used with a personal pronoun.

> She'll (she will) leave for Greece on Thursday.
> I'll (I will) leave the keys on the table by the front door.

b. In the past, *shall* was used in the 1st person (*I, we*) and *will* was used in the 2nd and 3rd person. Most people today, however, use *will* in all persons. *Shall* is used primarily in 1st person singular questions and in all persons for emphasis, warning, threat, or prohibition.

> Shall I leave the keys on the table?
> This travesty shall cease immediately! (an order)
> I shall return. (an emphatic promise)

c. Another way to express the future is to use *going to* + the simple form of the verb.

> She's going to leave for Greece on Thursday.
> We're going to meet him there next week.

d. The past tense of *going to* (*was going to, were going to*) is used to indicate an action that was planned or intended but that did not happen.

> I was going to call you, but I forgot.
> They were going to pick some raspberries, but it rained.

Perfect Tenses

These tenses (present perfect, past perfect, future perfect) are called perfect because they all refer to actions that have been completed (perfected) when the statement is made.

77. The present perfect tense (*have* or *has* + the past participle) describes an action in one of four ways:

a. an action that happened at some indefinite time in the past

> Raul *has learned* many new words.
> You *have done* well in school this year, haven't you?

b. an action that started in the past and is continuing into the present

> Peggy Grady *has worked* hard all her life.
> I've (I have) *lived* in Virginia since 1978.

c. an action that was repeated several times prior to the present

> It *has rained* every day this week.
> We*'ve* (we have) *seen* that movie five times.

d. an action completed so recently in the past that it still has an effect in the present

> He's not coming with us; he*'s been* sick all week.
> (This use of the present perfect indicates that he was sick and is still feeling the effects.)
> I'm so happy! I*'ve* just *found* my wallet!
> (This use of the present perfect indicates that the action is completed, but the joy of finding the wallet is still with the speaker.)

78. The choice between the simple past tense and the present perfect tense is one of intended meaning.

> Riza *ate* here often.
> (The past tense indicates that he doesn't eat here anymore. At one time he ate there, but not now.)
> Riza *has eaten* here often.
> (The present perfect tense indicates that he ate here in the past and he still eats here.)
> How long *did* you *study* French, Anna?
> (The past tense indicates that Anna once studied French, but that she no longer does.)
> How long *have* you *studied* French, Anna?
> (The present perfect tense indicates that Anna began studying French at some time in the past and that she probably still studies French.)

Exact times are used in specific patterns in these two tenses.

> Ali moved to Chicago last spring.
> Ali moved to Chicago eight months ago.
> Ali has lived in Chicago since last spring.
> Ali has lived in Chicago for eight months.

79. The past perfect tense describes an action completed or a condition existing prior to some other past event. It is used in conjunction with the past tense. It shows the time relationship between at least two events or conditions; that is, it shows that one event in the past occurred before another event in the past. It is formed by using *had* + the past participle of the verb.

> I *had* already *eaten* when you called last night.
> The show *had begun* when we arrived.

80. The future perfect tense describes a future act that will be completed before some other future time or event.

> They*'ll have eaten* by the time you arrive.
> By this time next week, Mike *will have finished* his term paper.

Progressive Tenses

These tenses (present progressive, past progressive, future progressive, present perfect progressive) are used to indicate that the action of the verb is continuous, not finished, at the time the statement is made.

81. The present progressive tense is used to express an activity that is happening at the present moment, or to describe future action.

> You *are reading* this page.
> I*'m writing*, right now.
> *Are* you *leaving* for Rome tomorrow?
> She*'s arriving* from Boston by train.

82. The past progressive tense describes a past action that was happening when another action interrupted or took place. It is used in conjunction with the past tense.

> I *was typing* when you called last night.
> You *were sleeping* when we came in.

83. The future progressive tense describes an action that will be happening when another future action happens.

> At this time next year, he*'ll be studying* at Cornell University.
> They *will be harvesting* the corn by the time you get there.

84. The present perfect progressive tense describes an action that began in the past and has continued up to the present. It can often be interchanged with the present perfect tense.

> Mike has been doing poor work recently.
> Mike has done poor work recently.

> Rollie and Dot have been working on their book since March.
> Rollie and Dot have worked on their book since March.

85. The past perfect progressive and the future perfect progressive tenses exist in theory, but they are rarely used. They are included in section 73 for reference.

> Ron *had been calling* me all day Saturday, but I wasn't home.
> Jennifer *will have been visiting* her grandmother in California for two weeks by the time I finish my last exam.

86. Do not shift tenses. Consistency is important in sentence structure.

> *wrong*: When she *arrives* home at night, I*'ll be* asleep.
> *right*: When she *arrives* home at night, I *am* asleep.

> *wrong*: I *stayed* home from work because I*'m* sick
> *right*: I *stayed* home from work because I *was* sick.

> *wrong*: What *did* she *say*? She *said* her name *is* Alissa.
> *right*: What *did* she *say*? She *said* her name *was* Alissa.
> *right*: What *did* she *say*? She *said*, "My name *is* Alissa."

If a sentence combines several tenses, their sequence must be logical.

> I *believed* you last year; I *believe* you now; I*'ll* always *believe* you.
> I *watched* TV yesterday; I*'m watching* it today, and I *shall watch* it tomorrow.

AUXILIARY VERBS

There are many auxiliary, or helping, verbs that are used with main verbs. Here are some of the most common:

must	need	let
may	might	can
should	would	could
shall	will	ought
have (has)	going to	do (does, did)
be (am, is, are, was, were, being, been)		

87. Auxiliary verbs are frequently contracted when used with pronouns. Contractions are customary and acceptable in all uses of American English. Here are some of the most common:

be:	I'm	you're	he's	she's	it's	we're	they're
shall/will:	I'll	you'll	he'll	she'll	it'll	we'll	they'll
have/has:	I've	you've	he's	she's	it's	we've	they've
had/would:	I'd	you'd	he'd	she'd	it'd	we'd	they'd
— have:	would've	could've	should've	might've	must've		

88. An auxiliary verb is never used with the past tense form of the main verb.

> *wrong*: I had began the exercise.
> *right*: I *had begun* the exercise.

> *wrong*: They could saw the lights.
> *right*: They *could see* the lights.

89. Always use the past participle form of the main verb when *have, has,* or *had* is used as an auxiliary. Never use the past participle alone as a verb.

wrong: I drunk the water.
right: I *had drunk* the water.

90. Some auxiliary verbs are also used as main verbs.

We all *need* love. (*main*)
You *need* not *go*. (*auxiliary*)
Alice *does* her work. (*main*)
She *doesn't want* our help. (*auxiliary*)
The Redskins football team *has* a new coach. (*main*)
He*'s lived* here all his life. (*auxiliary*)

91. Negatives are formed by placing *not* between the auxiliary verb and the main verb. Here is a list of the most common negative contractions:

isn't	weren't	hasn't
hadn't	don't	can't
won't	shouldn't	needn't
wasn't	aren't	haven't
doesn't	didn't	couldn't
wouldn't	mustn't	oughtn't

Peter has *not* eaten dinner.   Peter has*n't* eaten dinner.
You must *not* smoke.   You must*n't* smoke.

92. In complex sentences where the main verb is in the present tense, the present tense auxiliaries *may, can, shall,* and *will* are used in the dependent clause.

My boss *tells* me that I *may* get a 12-percent raise in pay.
Linda *thinks* that she*'ll* pass the exam.
Roberto *says* that he *can* fix the carburetor of the car.

In complex sentences where the main verb is in the past tense, the past tense auxiliaries *might, could, should,* and *would* are used in the dependent clause.

My boss *told* me that I *might* get a 12-percent raise in pay.
Linda *thought* that she*'d* pass the exam.
Roberto *said* that he *could* fix the carburetor of the car.

93. Of all the auxiliary verbs, only *have to* has a present, past, future, and perfect tense.

I have to slow down every time I drive on this road.
We had to slow down on this road last night.
You will have to slow down on this road tonight.
She has had to slow down on this road many times.

94. Tag endings ask questions or invite confirmation of some already known fact. They always contain a pronoun and a form of an auxiliary, but they do not contain a main verb. Negative tag endings are used after affirmative statements; affirmative tag endings are used after negative statements. The auxiliary is the same in the tag ending as in the statement.

> Clayton hasn't written to you yet, has he?
> Heather can drive a car now, can't she?
> They gave you what you wanted, didn't they?
> Tolkman won't be coming with us, will he?

95. Most direct questions in English are answered with short answers. Short answers are formed by adding the subject of the sentence to the auxiliary verb or the verb *be*, and by adding the word *yes* or *no*. The same auxiliary occurs in the question and the answer. The main verb is not repeated.

> Can he make an omelet? Yes, he can. No, he can't.
> Do you speak Chinese? Yes, I do. No, I don't.
> Will Laura marry Luke? Yes, she will. No, she won't.

In short answers, noun subjects are generally replaced by pronouns.

> Is Ms. Cassidine in class today? Yes, she is. No, she isn't.
> Can the house be built in a month? Yes, it can. No, it can't.

96. In sentences that express opposite situations, repetition is often avoided by using *but* and an auxiliary verb in the second thought. The main verb is not repeated. Note that these example sentences indicate contrast or contradiction, connecting affirmative and negative thoughts.

> Carol has eaten dinner, but Greg hasn't.
> (There is no need to repeat the full predicate—"Greg hasn't eaten dinner.")
> Hunter doesn't have to work tomorrow, but I do.
> Hassan can't speak Berber, but Brahin can.
> The police think that Betty Ann is a thief, but she says she isn't.
> The first level won't be difficult, but the second will.

97. In sentences that express similarities, repetition is often avoided by using *and* with *too, so, either,* or *neither* and an auxiliary verb in the second thought. The main verb is not repeated. Note that the first group of example sentences connects affirmative statements or thoughts, while the second group connects negative statements or thoughts.

> Tasha lives in Moscow, and Ivan does too.
> (There is no need to repeat the full predicate—"Ivan lives in Moscow.")
> I went to school in Ann Arbor, and so did Rory.
> Gerry can row a boat, and so can Alan.
> Lorraine is from New York, and her husband is too.

Alfonso rarely travels outside of Spain, and neither does his brother.
(There is no need to repeat the full predicate—"his brother doesn't travel outside of Spain.")
Chuck doesn't play backgammon, and Shirley doesn't either.
We won't attend her wedding, and Erica won't either.
Nora can't pedal her old bike, and neither can Winnie.

98. Rejoinders are short responses to statements. They are usually modeled on the statement, and they use an auxiliary verb with *either, neither, so,* or *too.*

Grace loves baseball. So do I.
Liz can make good cocktails. So can Peg.
Harry is getting fat. I am too.
She hasn't read Gore Vidal's new novel. Neither have I.
Terry doesn't want to miss this radio show. I don't either.

99. Auxiliary verbs may be omitted if they are in the same form as other verbs in the sentence.

We will remember the good times and will forget the bad ones.

Since the flow of this sentence shows that the thoughts (actions) are closely related, the second auxiliary verb can be omitted.

We will remember the good times and forget the bad ones.

100. Clauses using the construction *as . . . as* are generally followed by only the subject and the auxiliary when the verbs in the two elements of the sentence are the same.

We drove as far as we could. (drive)
She spends as much time with her father as she can. (spend with him)

101. Clauses that begin with *so that* usually use the auxiliaries *can/could, will/would,* or *may/might* to express cause, purpose, or reason for an effect or result.

We cut her bangs short so that she could see better.
They climbed the tower so that they might look upon the entire city.
Susan dieted strictly so that she would maintain her health.

102. Ability and capability: *can* shows ability, while *be able to* shows capability.

You can ride that horse. (You have the ability.)
No, I can't; I'm not able to do it.
I know you are able to ride; I taught you.

103. **Advisability:** *had better* indicates the advisability of an action. This auxiliary is followed by the simple form of the verb and is often contracted *'d better*.

He'd better not see her anymore.
You'd better notify his relatives that he is sick.

Note that *had better* refers to future time, even though it appears to be a past form.

104. **Causatives:** *have* or *get* + the past participle, and *make* + the simple form of the verb, may be used to indicate the cause of some action or performance.

He made the dog lie down and close its eyes.
Will your mother make you wear brown shoes?
Did you have your heater checked before the winter?
Richie has his suits pressed once a month.
Darlene got her car washed last week.
If the repairman comes today, have him fix the oven.
   (Since this is a subjunctive mood sentence, *fix* is used after *have*.)

105. **Conclusions:** *must have* + the past participle is used to conclude something about past occurrences or to project high probability that an event will occur.

It's very cold; the temperature must have dropped 40 degrees.
The picture just went black; the TV must've broken.
You must have felt terrible when you heard the bad news.

106. **Customary action:** *would* + the simple form of the verb is used to express habitual or customary action.

Every year on November 1 he would start to grow a beard.
In the spring, he'd shave it off.

107. **Determination:** *do, does, did, shall,* and *will* are all used to express determination, emphasis, promise, or threat in otherwise simple indicative mood statements. (See also **74; 76.**)

I do know her.
   (This is a stronger, more emphatic statement than *I know her*.)
You will come home by 11:00.
   (This is a courteous command when addressed to a specific person; the speaker is determined.)
This meeting shall come to order.
   (This statement seems almost threatening when the speaker tells the audience to stop talking.)

108. Discontinued action: *used to* and *would* describe repeated, habitual, or customary actions that happened over a period of time in the past, but that no longer do.

> We used to live in New York.
> Alaska is a change for Sue; she's used to living in Turkey.
> I remember that every Monday Professor Alban would give us a test; on Tuesdays we would go over it in class.
> I used to smoke, but I stopped. I was used to running, and I wanted to continue.

109. Expectation: *be supposed to* + the simple form of the verb is used to express anticipation or expectation.

> We are supposed to know this material by Friday. (*present*)
> The bus is supposed to be here by now. (*present*)
> The plane was supposed to land an hour ago. (*past*)
> You were supposed to meet me. Where were you? (*past*)

Another term that expresses expectation is *should have* + the past participle.

> We should have known this material by last Friday.
> The bus should have been here by now.
> The plane should have landed an hour ago.

110. Invitations: *would like* + the infinitive means "want" or "desire."

> We would like to learn to play chess.
> I would like to go out to dinner tonight.
> Would you like to go out with me to a movie?
> Would you like to watch a movie on TV?

111. Necessity: *need* + a gerund or *need to be* + a past participle expresses necessity.

> This electrical system needs rewiring.
> These electrical systems need to be rewired.

> Those vegetables need reheating before we can serve them.
> That vegetable needs to be reheated before we can serve it.

112. Present necessity may also be expressed by *must, have to, ought to,* or *should* + the simple form of the verb. Past necessity may be expressed by *had to* + the simple form of the verb, or *ought to have* or *should have* + the past participle.

> You must slow your pace or you'll tire early.
> I have to prepare this project by tomorrow.

We ought to finish this; we've been working on it for three weeks.
Paul should lose weight; he's much too heavy.
You had to leave early last night, didn't you?
Yvonne ought to have completed her thesis by now.
We should've listened more carefully to your instructions.

113. Obligation: *should, must, ought,* and *have to* express obligation. Only *ought* may be followed by an infinitive.

> You should know better than to walk in poison ivy.
> You should have known better than to have stayed up all night.
> We ought to change the oil in our car.
> You must return all those books to the library.
> I have to work this weekend; I'm behind in my programming.

114. Permission: *may* + the simple form of the verb indicates permission. *Let* + the simple form of the verb + an objective case pronoun is also used to express permission.

> You may enter now. (You are allowed to go in.)
> May I leave? (Am I permitted to depart?)
> Will you let me use your car this afternoon?
> The Andersons let us fish in their lake last summer.

115. Possible future action: *may* + the simple form of the verb indicates a possibility in the future.

> We may go to the theater tomorrow; we haven't decided yet.
> If we sell all our produce, we may be able to buy a new car.

116. Possibility and probability: *may, might, could,* and *would* + the simple form of the verb all express some degree of possibility or probability. (See also **105**.)

> If I didn't have to work tonight, I would attend your lecture.
> Doris would be happier if she moved back home.
> I could ask the Lewises to the party if you wanted me to.
> I may take my vacation in Mexico this year.
> Ted might move his house boat to a new mooring.
> It might snow; you'd better dress warmly.

117. Preference: *would rather* + the simple form of the verb means "prefer," and is often contracted *'d rather.*

> I'd rather go to a museum than watch TV.
> Would you rather live in Rio or São Paulo?

Would rather have + the past participle indicates a past preference that was unfulfilled.

> I'm sorry I went to the game. It was so crowded there. I would rather have stayed home and watched it on TV.

118. Suggestion: *could, might, should,* and *had better* + the simple form of the verb are all used for present or future suggestions.

> Next semester you could take World History. You might also take Modern Civics, and you should take a science elective. Above all, you'd better take Philosophy 101.

VERBALS

The three types of verbals (infinitives, gerunds, and participles) all have rules governing their uses. Here are some of the more important ones.

119. Use an infinitive after *asked, said,* and *told* to indicate commands, requests, or invitations. *Said* is never immediately followed by a noun or pronoun, although *asked* and *told* often are.

> They asked me to write a speech.
> She told Juan to behave more courteously.
> Jimmy said to keep the information to ourselves.
> They said not to hurry because we had plenty of time.
> Trisha asked us not to forget her daughter's birthday.
> Has Senator Pell asked you to attend the fund-raising dinner?

120. Both the subject and the object of an infinitive are objective case.

> Mr. Lazarus wanted me to work for him.
> She asked us to visit her.

121. Avoid splitting infinitives except when the construction would be awkward.

> *wrong*: They asked us to quickly hand in our papers.
> *right*:   They asked us to hand in our papers quickly.

> *wrong*: I have to unfortunately tell you some bad news.
> *right*:   Unfortunately, I have to tell you some bad news.

However, note: Our parents taught us to always say "Thank you."

122. Never use an infinitive after *make*. Use the simple form of the verb.

Mrs. Backsler makes her sons do their homework after school.
They made me do it; I didn't want to.

123. Here is a list of commonly used verbs that are followed by infinitives. Note the placement of the pronouns in some of the sentences.

advise:	Mohammed advised her to rent a car for a week.
care:	She didn't care to attend the performance.
cause:	Piper caused us to be late.
command:	The soldier on guard duty commanded us to halt.
decide:	Sam decided not to bake cookies for the fair.
deserve:	I felt I deserved to win the blue ribbon.
encourage:	They've been encouraging us to study engineering.
force:	Time pressures are forcing us to cancel some of our plans.
forget:	Did you forget to send her a birthday card?
get:	Try to get him to agree to Walker's offer, will you?
hope:	We hope to have seen her by this time next month.
instruct:	We were instructed to leave as quietly as possible.
invite:	I'd like to invite you to see my newest painting.
know how:	Are you sure that she knows how to ski?
	If I knew how to drive, I'd help you.
learn:	Saul is learning to sail a catamaran.
mean:	I didn't mean to say that; it just came out of my mouth.
order:	The police officer ordered the suspect to raise his hands.
persuade:	How can I persuade you to change your mind?
plan:	We're planning to leave as soon as you're able.
promise:	If you promise not to blab, I'll tell you a secret.
remind:	Have you reminded Sylvia to send the telegram?
teach:	Who taught Billie Jean King to play tennis?
tell:	Tell Mitchell to stop playing the piano and come to lunch.
urge:	Joey urged us to put our house on the market at a higher price.
warn:	The sign warns everyone to "Watch your step."

124. Since gerunds are nouns, use the possessive case when appropriate. (See also **17**; **42**.)

Her resigning dismayed us.
Marilyn's scheming was the talk of the office.

125. Here is a list of commonly used verbs that may be followed only by gerunds (no other verbal).

admit:	Cheryl admitted taking Debby's coat.
appreciate:	Mom would appreciate hearing from you.
avoid:	We have avoided telling her the news.

consider:	Joyce is considering buying Jerry's car.
deny:	Howard denied losing the book.
enjoy:	We always enjoy visiting Gene in Connecticut.
escape:	Did he escape being captured by the enemy?
finish:	Please finish typing the report as soon as you can.
imagine:	Imagine body surfing in Hawaii!
keep:	Keep trying; you're bound to succeed.
miss:	Unfortunately, I missed meeting the conductor after the concert.
postpone:	I had to postpone going to the dentist until my cold was better.
practice:	I wish you wouldn't practice kicking the ball in the house.
quit:	We quit smoking on March 24.
resent:	Kristin resents having to do all the cooking in her family.
resist:	Why has John resisted buying a new car when his old one is so bad?
suggest:	Does the reviewer suggest seeing or skipping that movie?
stop:	You've got to stop driving so fast!

The expressions *do you mind* and *would you mind* are also followed by gerunds.

Do you mind living in the country?
Would you mind holding this for me?

126. Some verbs may be followed by either an infinitive or a gerund.

begin:	The rain began to fall.
	The rain began falling.
can't bear:	I can't bear to watch the so-called sport of boxing.
	I can't bear watching the so-called sport of boxing.
can't stand:	I can't stand to listen to his boring stories.
	I can't stand listening to his boring stories.
continue:	We continued to play cards during lunch.
	We continued playing cards during lunch.
like:	I like to visit Grandma on the eastern shore.
	I like visiting Grandma on the eastern shore.
neglect:	She neglected to tell him that his mother had called.
	She neglected telling him that his mother had called.
prefer:	Has he always preferred to bake his own bread?
	Has he always preferred baking his own bread?
start:	Does Natalie start to teach tomorrow?
	Does Natalie start teaching tomorrow?

127. For expressing purpose, an infinitive is used when the meaning is "in order to"; a gerund is used after "for."

> The boots were made to walk in. (in order to walk in them)
> The boots were made for walking.
> Can you use this herb for brewing tea?
> Have you used this tool to fix your car? (in order to fix it)

128. Participles may be present (speaking), past (spoken), or perfect (having spoken). As adjectives, participles must modify nouns or pronouns. Take care not to let a participle dangle, that is, hang loosely in a sentence without a clearly defined noun or pronoun to modify. It is usually best to place the participle close to its noun or pronoun.

> *wrong*: Jumping to the ground, my keys fell out.
> *right*: Jumping to the ground, I lost my keys.
> (It was *I* who jumped to the ground, not the keys; the participle must modify *I*.)

> *wrong*: By taking this short cut, time can be saved.
> *right*: By taking this short cut, you can save time.

VERBS AS COMPLEMENTS

129. Many verbs function in a complement form. They frequently require certain specific words or forms following them. Note the patterns of *that* clauses, infinitives, gerunds, pronoun placements, etc., in these selected examples.

> The panel asked that Judge O'Conner explain her position on juvenile rights.
> They asked her to clarify her previous statement.
> They urged that she be forthright and honest.
> They suggested that she relax and take her time.
> She decided that she would meet with the senators.
> She decided to talk to them one by one.
> She hoped that she could gain their confidence.
> Most expected that she would "sail" through the hearings.
> Many expected her to encounter little opposition.
> Eleanor promised Franklin that she would write often.
> She promised to keep him up to date on her activities while she was away.
> He reminded her that she shouldn't forget her pills.
> She admitted that she often forgot them.
> She recalled that he often forgot his own pills.
> He denied that he forgot.
> My wife had me wax the floor today.
> Yesterday, she got me to clean it.

Tomorrow, she wants to get the rugs cleaned.
Next week, she'll have someone paint the walls.
She heard the wind blow.
She heard the leaves rustling.
I can't make you tell me your name, little boy.
Please let me put this coat around you.
We want to help you find your parents.
I'm sure they're looking forward to finding you, too.
Do you object to sitting here in my office till we find them?
It seems likely that they'll know where to look for you.
It happens that I see them coming now.

EXERCISES
(Answers are on pages 107–109.)

A. Circle the word or words in parentheses that make the sentence correct.

1. Mr. Olsen's watch (*is lying, is laying*) on the desk.

2. The President said, "It is vital to our interests that we (*are, be*) represented at the peace talks."

3. If you finish on time, (*we'll, we'd*) be surprised.

4. I wish Terri (*were, had been*) more honest when she wrote her résumé.

5. If I (*was, were*) you and were younger, I'd try it.

6. The principal parts of the verb *win* are win, (*wan, won*), winning, and won.

7. The mail had already come when Jim (*called, had called*).

8. Secretary Watt has been (*changed, changing*) many of his predecessor's policies.

9. "Zachary," his mother called, "you (*must'nt, mustn't*) leave the screen door open; flies will get in."

10. She understands that unless she studies (*she'll, she'd*) fail the exam.

11. Gallagher won't sign the contract, (*won't, will*) he?

12. Mr. Colvin is a good speller, but Mr. Mallory (*can't, isn't*).

13. Keith is a good skier, and (*so, too*) is Danielle.

14. They buried the coins so that no one else (*would know, knew*) where they were.

15. You'd better not (*to swim, swim*) in that dirty creek.

16. I don't understand it; Mary should (*have called, called*) us an hour ago.

17. We may (*buy, to buy*) a new typewriter for our office.

18. Susan (*said me, said*) not to tell anyone that she was getting a raise.

19. Ms. Kessler is going to teach Linda (*playing, to play*) the viola.

20. When are you going to start (*dancing, danced*) again?

21. Fred suggested that Ethel (*drinks, drink*) milk to calm her.

B. Circle the term in parentheses that makes the sentence correct.

1. She (*lay, laid*) her new rug on the den floor.

2. He (*raised, rose*) from his bed feeling well rested.

3. Please (*sit, set*) the pitcher on the table.

4. We will be (*glad, gladly*) to see you.

5. Your casserole smells (*wonderful, wonderfully*).

6. If this proves (*wrong, wrongly*), we'll be embarrassed.

7. Hey, Sandy, do you want to help me carry this, (*please., please?*)

8. If I have the money, (*I'd, I'll*) travel to India this summer.

9. I wish this (*was, were*) Saturday; I can't wait!

10. It is essential that Daphne (*keep, keeps*) her job.

11. If I had the money, I (*would travel, will travel*) to India this summer.

12. It is necessary that he (*finishes, finish*) his education before entering the Army.

13. The professor insisted that she (*be, is*) on time for every class.

14. If I had had the money, I'd (*travel, have traveled*) to India last summer.

15. I've (*spoken, spoke*) to Mr. Cousteau several times by telephone.

16. She said she (*swam, had swam*) the channel yesterday.

C. Fill in the missing principal parts of the verbs in the table below.

	Present	*Past*	*Progressive*	*Past Participle* (with *have* or *has*)
1.	_____	_____	singing	_____
2.	_____	_____	_____	spent
3.	_____	fought	_____	_____
4.	break	_____	_____	_____
5.	take	_____	_____	_____
6.	_____	knew	_____	_____
7.	_____	_____	_____	put
8.	_____	_____	_____	finished
9.	_____	_____	becoming	_____
10.	_____	began	_____	_____
11.	think	_____	_____	_____
12.	_____	_____	polishing	_____
13.	fix	_____	_____	_____
14.	_____	met	_____	_____
15.	_____	_____	costing	_____

	Present	Past	Progressive	Past Participle (with *have* or *has*)
16.	_____	_____	leaving	_____
17.	_____	_____	_____	spoken
18.	_____	_____	_____	held
19.	_____	wondered	_____	_____
20.	run	_____	_____	_____

D. Write the verb in each of the following sentences in the indicated tense and voice.

Example: The dog (*cry*) all morning.

(*past, active*): _____cried_____

1. I (*watch*) this TV show for the past hour.
   (*present perfect progressive, active*): _____

2. Polly (*depend*) on Kathleen to wake her up on time.
   (*future, active*): _____

3. Florence (*meet*) Julian before she met George.
   (*past perfect, active*): _____

4. It (*say*) that chicken soup is good for a common cold.
   (*present perfect, passive*): _____

5. When we got there the store (*close*).
   (*past, passive*): _____

6. This program (*monitor*) by the people in the control booth.
   (*present progressive, passive*): _____

7. Janie (*open*) her presents when Pete arrived.
   (*past progressive, active*): _____

8. I (*make*) the coffee by the time you all awaken.
   (*future perfect, active*): _____

9. By this time next week, they (*drive*) through Canada.

   (*future progressive, active*): _____

10. According to Eleanor's letter, the bus (*arrive*) at 8:30.

    (*present, active*): _____

11. The room we were supposed to stay in (*paint*).

    (*past progressive, passive*): _____

12. That story (*read*) by the editor before it gets printed.

    (*future, passive*): _____

13. The Taylors (*move*) to Williamsburg in 1981.

    (*past, active*): _____

14. The Taylors (*live*) in Williamsburg since 1981.

    (*present perfect, active*): _____

E. Write the verb in the indicated person, number, tense, and voice.

   Example: (*hear*) 3rd person, singular, future, passive:

   he (she, it) will be heard _____

   1. (*toss*) 2nd person, plural, present progressive, active:

      _____

   2. (*carry*) 1st person, singular, future perfect, passive:

      _____

   3. (*plant*) 3rd person, plural, present perfect, passive:

      _____

   4. (*operate*) 2nd person, singular, past, active:

      _____

5. (*call*) 1st person, plural, past perfect, active:

_____

6. (*call*) 1st person, plural, past perfect, passive:

_____

7. (*signal*) 3rd person, singular, past progressive, passive:

_____

8. (*drive*) 2nd person, singular, future, active:

_____

9. (*drive*) 2nd person, plural, future perfect, active:

_____

10. (*steal*) 3rd person, plural, present progressive, passive:

_____

11. (*tear*) 3rd person, singular, present perfect, active:

_____

12. (*tear*) 3rd person, singular, present perfect progressive, active:

_____

13. (*bring*) 1st person, singular, past, passive:

_____

14. (*bring*) 1st person, singular, past progressive, active:

_____

15. (*know*) 3rd person, plural, present, passive:

_____

16. (*forget*) 1st person, plural, future progressive, active:

_____

F. Each of the following sentences contains an unnecessary shift in mood, tense, or voice. Underline the verb that needs to be changed and write its correct form in the space provided.

Example: Yesterday she came to my apartment and <u>asks</u> to borrow some sugar.   _____*asked*_____

1. She wished she were older or he was younger.   _____

2. Meredith put the fruit in the basket and a ribbon was tied around it.   _____

3. Grandma always sets the table before the guests will arrive.   _____

4. After you have read the recipe, then get out the cooking utensils; now you have been ready to mix the ingredients.   _____

5. The leaves will be changing color soon, and the weather turns cold.   _____

6. If I were you and was worried, I'd call a doctor.   _____

7. Maureen thought she'll lose weight, but she didn't.   _____

8. If I had run faster, I would win the race.   _____

9. The player kicked the ball and was run after it.   _____

10. The Senate discussed the merits of the treaty, and then it was passed.   _____

11. If you hurry, you arrive before the show starts.   _____

12. Harry says he might go to Seattle today.   _____

G. Write the contraction for each of the following verb phrases in the space provided.

Example: I am   __*I'm*__

   1. we shall   _____

   2. she has   _____

   3. it would   _____

   4. you have   _____

   5. might have   _____

   6. they had   _____

   7. he is   _____

   8. must not   _____

   9. can not   _____

  10. should not   _____

  11. you will   _____

  12. do not   _____

  13. will not   _____

  14. they are   _____

H. Complete each of the following sentences with an appropriate word (an auxiliary verb or *too, so, either, neither*) or with a tag ending, a short answer, or a rejoinder.

Example: He wanted to go, but he _____*couldn't*_____ .

   1. They pushed the cart as far as they _____ .

   2. She's already read today's newspaper, _____ ?

   3. Carrie doesn't like to work too hard. I don't

     _____ .

   4. Is Mrs. Carrington a dentist? Yes, _____ .

   5. Hollis lives in Texas and _____ does Clayton.

   6. This mountain will be difficult to climb, but the next one

     _____ .

   7. I think we should drive as far as we _____ today.

   8. Mai Ling can play the piano. _____ I.

9. Eddie can't go with us today, and _____ can Ruth.

10. Andy drives an old car, and Larry does _____.

11. I haven't seen that new play, but my husband

_____.

12. My wife thinks this tie is old-fashioned, but I say it

_____.

13. Was that office building here last year? No,

_____.

14. Do you always think before you speak? Yes,

_____.

15. You didn't put paint over that wallpaper,

- _____?

16. Dorothy will be joining us for lunch, _____?

I. Circle the auxiliary verb in parentheses that makes the sentence correct.

1. We trimmed the hedges so that more sunlight (*can, could*) get through.

2. The reason for the tax cut was so that more money (*may, might*) be available.

3. You (*'d better, better*) tone up your muscles if you want to try out for gymnastics this year.

4. Every time one of us kids lost a tooth, my grandfather (*would give, gave*) us 25¢.

5. I don't care what the other parents let their children do, you (*will, are*) come home right after band practice.

6. Angela lives in Minnesota now; she (*used to, did*) live in Alabama.

7. Will they (*make, do*) you cut your hair if you join the Air Force?

8. I (*may have, must have*) fallen asleep early last night; I don't remember anything after 10:00.

9. Who (*may, is supposed to*) teach the chemistry course this year?

10. I (*'d like, 'll like*) to have a dinner party for all my friends.

11. This dress (*needs, would like*) ironing; it's much too wrinkled to wear.

12. You (*might, ought to*) take off your coat; it's going to be warm in the conference room.

13. Kunta (*has to, should to*) stay up all night to finish his assignment.

14. Charles (*will, may*) trade in his car for a motorcycle; he's not sure yet.

15. "Mother, I want to go over to David's house." "You (*can, may*) go if you're home by 5 o'clock."

16. It sounds as though you want to save money on repairs. You (*can, could*) take a course on self-repair, you know.

J. Write the appropriate form of the verb (simple, past participle, infinitive, or gerund) in each of the following sentences.

Example: (*shine*) Be sure to have your shoes _____*shined*_____ before your interview.

1. (*visit*) Patricia said she really enjoyed_____

Atlantic City this past summer.

2. (*go*) I would rather_____to the mountains

than to the beach.

3. (*see*) Phyllis hoped_____the Hearst museum

on her trip.

4. (*leave*) Dan must have _____ already; I don't see his car.

5. (*read*) You really ought _____ this book; you'll love it.

6. (*walk*) I prefer _____ in my garden in the morning when the air is cool.

7. (*ride*) Mary asked if we would like _____ to work in her car today.

8. (*wash*) Do these towels need to be _____ ?

9. (*operate*) Joan is learning _____ the snow-mobile.

10. (*blow*) Please stop _____ smoke in my face.

11. (*study*) "I should have _____ harder when I was in school," Tony said.

12. (*use*) Claudia let us _____ her typewriter.

13. (*make*) This pan can be used for _____ crepes.

14. (*anticipate*) You should have _____ trouble when you first heard the funny noise in the engine.

15. (*open*) Rose may _____ a travel agency.

16. (*attend*) Frances invited us _____ the opening of the new exhibit.

17. (*dance*) Tara loves to imagine _____ with the New York City Ballet.

18. (*name*) Karen may _____ her baby "Theo-

dore."

19. (*get up*) We were supposed to _____ at 6:30,

but we overslept.

20. (*hold*) Would you mind _____ the baby while

I put my coat on.

K. Review section **129**, then circle the term in parentheses that makes the sentence correct.

1. Mother always hoped that I (*become, would become*) a lawyer.

2. Our teacher wants to have someone (*erase, to erase*) the chalkboard.

3. It seemed likely that he (*will survive, would survive*) the ordeal.

4. Dwayne said he wanted to help us (*prune, pruning*) the rose bushes.

5. Her uncle asked that she (*meets, meet*) him for lunch.

6. He asked her (*meet, to meet*) him at 12:15.

7. The defendant denied that he (*did, didn't do*) the crime.

8. We expected that you (*were, would be*) late.

9. We expected you (*to be, were*) late.

10. The sign reads, "Please let the elderly (*sit, to sit*) in these seats."

ANSWER KEY

The number in parentheses after an answer refers to the rule in this section that covers this point.

A.
1. is lying (55; 72)
2. be (63)
3. we'll (64*a*)
4. had been (65)
5. were (63; 68)
6. won (72)
7. called (79)
8. changing (84)
9. mustn't (91)
10. she'll (92)
11. will (94)
12. isn't (95)
13. so (97)
14. would know (101)
15. swim (103)
16. have called (109)
17. buy (115)
18. said (119)
19. to play (123)
20. dancing (126)
21. drink (129)

B.
1. laid (54; 72)
2. rose (55; 72)
3. set (54; 72)
4. glad (56*a*)
5. wonderful (56*b*)
6. wrong (56*c*)
7. please. (59)
8. I'll (64*a*)
9. were (60; 63)
10. keep (62)
11. would travel (64*b*)
12. finish (67)
13. be (67)
14. have traveled (64*c*)
15. spoken (72; 89)
16. swam (72; 88)

C. All of the answers in this exercise refer to rule **72.**

	Present	*Past*	*Progressive*	*Past Participle*
1.	sing	sang	singing	sung
2.	spend	spent	spending	spent
3.	fight	fought	fighting	fought
4.	break	broke	breaking	broken
5.	take	took	taking	taken
6.	know	knew	knowing	known
7.	put	put	putting	put
8.	finish	finished	finishing	finished
9.	become	became	becoming	become
10.	begin	began	beginning	begun
11.	think	thought	thinking	thought
12.	polish	polished	polishing	polished
13.	fix	fixed	fixing	fixed
14.	meet	met	meeting	met
15.	cost	cost	costing	cost
16.	leave	left	leaving	left
17.	speak	spoke	speaking	spoken
18.	hold	held	holding	held
19.	wonder	wondered	wondering	wondered
20.	run	ran	running	run

D.
1. have been watching (**73; 84**)
2. will depend (**73; 76**)
3. had met (**73; 79**)
4. has been said (**73; 77**)
5. was closed (**73; 75**)
6. is being monitored (**73; 81**)
7. was opening (**73; 82**)
8. will have made (**73; 80**)
9. will be driving (**73; 83**)
10. arrives (**73; 74d**)
11. was being painted (**73; 82**)
12. will be read (**73; 76**)
13. moved (**73; 75; 78**)
14. have lived (**73; 75; 78**)

E. All of the answers in this exercise refer to rule **73**.

1. you are tossing
2. I will have been carried
3. they have been planted
4. you operated
5. we had called
6. we had been called
7. he (she, it) was being signaled
8. you will drive
9. you will have driven
10. they are being stolen
11. he (she, it) has torn
12. he (she, it) has been tearing
13. I was brought
14. I was bringing
15. they are known
16. we will be forgetting

F.

Incorrect form	*Correct form*
1. was	were (**68**)
2. a ribbon was tied	tied a ribbon (**71**)
3. will arrive	arrive (**86**)
4. have been	are (**86**)
5. turns	will be turning/will turn (**86**)
6. was	were (**68**)
7. she'll	she'd (**92**)
8. win	have won (**64c**)
9. was run	ran (**71**)
10. it was passed	passed it (**71**)
11. arrive	will arrive (**64a**)
12. might	may (**92**)

G. All of the answers in this exercise refer to rules **87** and **91**.

1. we'll
2. she's
3. it'd
4. you've
5. might've
6. they'd
7. he's
8. mustn't
9. can't
10. shouldn't
11. you'll
12. don't
13. won't
14. they're

H.
1. could (**100**)
2. hasn't she (**94**)
3. either (**98**)
4. she is (**95**)
5. so (**97**)
6. won't (**96**)
7. can (**100**)
8. So can (**98**)
9. neither (**97**)
10. too (**97**)
11. has (**96**)
12. isn't (**96**)
13. it wasn't (**95**)
14. I do (**95**)
15. did you (**94**)
16. won't she (**94**)

I.
1. could (**101**)
2. might (**101**)
3. 'd better (**103**)
4. would give (**106**)
5. will (**107**)
6. used to (**108**)
7. make (**104**)
8. must have (**105**)
9. is supposed to (**109**)
10. 'd like (**110**)
11. needs (**111**)
12. ought to (**112**)
13. has to (**113**)
14. may (**115**)
15. may (**114**)
16. could (**118**)

J.
1. visiting (**125**)
2. go (**117**)
3. to see (**123**)
4. left (**104**)
5. to read (**113**)
6. to walk/walking (**126**)
7. to ride (**110**)
8. washed (**111**)
9. to operate (**123**)
10. blowing (**125**)
11. studied (**112**)
12. use (**114**)
13. making (**127**)
14. anticipated (**109**)
15. open (**115**)
16. to attend (**123**)
17. dancing (**125**)
18. name (**116**)
19. get up (**109**)
20. holding (**125**)

K.
1. would become (**129**)
2. erase (**129**)
3. would survive (**92; 129**)
4. prune (**129**)
5. meet (**129**)
6. to meet (**129**)
7. did (**129**)
8. would be (**129**)
9. to be (**129**)
10. sit (**129**)

Adjectives, Adverbs, and Articles

130. Many adverbs are formed from adjectives by adding *ly* to the adjectives.

a. Note the spelling changes in some of these examples.

Adjective	*Adverb*	*Adjective*	*Adverb*
accidental	accidentally	noticeable	noticeably
beautiful	beautifully	official	officially
careful	carefully	soft	softly
clear	clearly	temporary	temporarily
happy	happily	true	truly
knowledgeable	knowledgeably	whole	wholly

b. Some words that end in *ly* are adjectives.

lowly   friendly   motherly

c. Some adverbs have two possible forms.

close	closely		fair	fairly
hard	hardly		high	highly

Drive close to the side of the road and watch closely for the street sign.

d. Some words may be used as adjectives or adverbs with no change in form.

fast   hard   low   late

The golfer hit the ball *low* and *hard*. (*adverbs*)
Unser is a *hard* driver in a *fast* car. (*adjectives*)

131. Do not confuse adjectival phrases with adverbial phrases. Since *due* is an adjective, the phrase *due to* should be used only to introduce an adjectival modifier.

She was late because she had a headache. (*adverbial*)
Her lateness was due to her headache. (*adjectival*)
He failed the exam because he didn't study. (*adverbial*)
His failure was due to the fact that he didn't study. (*adjectival*)

132. Do not use two negative adjectives or adverbs in the same construction.

a. *No* and *not* are the most common words used to make a sentence negative.

wrong: Suzanne doesn't have no car.
right: Suzanne doesn't have a car.
right: Suzanne has no car.

b. Some adverbs, such as *barely, never, rarely, scarcely,* and *seldom,* always make their sentences negative. Do not add *no* or *not* to sentences using these words.

> *wrong*: He doesn't never remember to close the door.
> *right*: He never remembers to close the door.
> *right*: He doesn't ever remember to close the door.

c. It is acceptable to use a construction such as *not unfamiliar* to mean *familiar.*

> I was aware of your difficulties.
> I was not unaware of your difficulties.

133. Do not use *when* or *where* to introduce noun clauses; they should be used as adverbs.

> They told us we could begin when we wanted.
> Tom always worked where he was told.

> *wrong*: FSU is the school where they go.
> *right*: FSU is the school that they are attending.

134. When the past participle of a verb is used as an adjective, the noun modified by that adjective is the receiver of some action.

> I have closed the window. The closed window rattled.

When the progressive (sometimes called the present participle) form of a verb is used as an adjective, the noun modified by that adjective is the giver, doer, actor, or instigator of some action.

> The dog barks a lot. The barking dog annoys us.
> To be an interesting person, one must be an interested person.

135. Numbering adjectives are either cardinal (one book, two geese, twelve months, fifty states) or ordinal (the first day, the second time, the twelfth night, the fiftieth book). (See also **150.**)

136. Use commas to separate adjectives of equal rank that precede nouns. Do not use commas if the adjectives qualify other adjectives as well as nouns. These example sentences are all correctly punctuated.

> Her lofty, inflated, obscure language confused us.
> She drove a flashy, red sports car.
> It was a brave, stupid, and reckless act.

Note that the comma comes before *and* in the last example.

137. Use hyphens with compound adjectives that precede nouns. Compound adjectives are two or more words that act together with the force of a single modifier. The singular form of a measurement is used as an adjective.

> He used a self-instructional manual to learn typing.
> The sign said that this would be a one-time-only sale.
> We drove north-northwest to get to Alberta.
> The Dallas-Ft. Worth airport is quite modern.
> The well-known actor dressed only in up-to-date fashions.
> a ten-foot ladder   a 16-pound turkey   a 30-day month

But note: The actor was well known. His fashions were up to date.

CONFUSING PAIRS

There are several pairs of adjectives and adverbs that native speakers of English often confuse in ordinary speech. Take care not to confuse them yourself, as the TOEFL requires that you know their correct usage.

138. *Almost* means "very nearly" or "not quite."
Most refers to the greater or greatest number.

> Almost everyone in our class owns a dictionary.
> You'll find that reference in most encyclopedias.

139. *Already* means "by this time" or "previously"; it occurs in affirmative statements and in questions.
Yet means "so far"; it occurs in negative statements and in questions.

> We've already been to Germany three times, but we haven't seen the Berlin Wall yet.
> Have you met my sister yet? No, not yet.
> Haven't we already met? You look familiar.

140. *Any* is used in negative statements and in questions that anticipate negative answers. (See also **40.**)
Some is used in affirmative statements and in questions that anticipate affirmative answers.

> I don't have any money with me.
> I can lend you some money.
> Do you want any bananas? No, I don't want any.
> Do you want some bananas? Yes, I do.

141. *Anymore* refers to something in the past that is no longer going on. It occurs at the end of negative statements and questions.
Still refers to continuous action that is going on up to the present. It occurs in both affirmative and negative statements and in questions, usually before the main verb, but after the verb *be*.

> Are you still at Yale? No, I'm not there anymore.
> Aren't you dancing anymore? No, it takes up too much time, but I'm still exercising every day.
> She doesn't still live in Athens, does she? No, not anymore.

142. *Farther* and *farthest* refer to distance or remoteness in space; that is, physical distance.
Further and *furthest* refer to distance in time, degree, extent, or quantity.

> Maine is farther from here than I thought.
> Montreal is the farthest we've gone on a vacation.
> Who went the furthest in school, you or your sisters?
> If you need further assistance, please ask that salesperson over there.

143. *Fewer* refers to items that can be counted.
Less refers to abstract and to noncountable items.

> Our old car uses less gas than our new one.
> It takes fewer gallons of gas to go the same distance.
> I spend less time on my assignments than Leslie does.
> I spend fewer hours per day on them than she does.
> This year's group seems to be eating fewer sandwiches and less fruit than last year's.

144. *Good* is always an adjective.
Well is usually an adverb describing how something is done; occasionally it is an adjective, meaning "healthy."

> This soup is good; it looks good and tastes good, too.
> You cook well, and you're a good worker. You dress well, too.
> I hope you're feeling well (healthy).

145. *Many* is used with plural countable nouns.
Much is used with abstract and with noncountable nouns.
The phrase *a lot of* is used interchangeably with *much* and *many*.

> Do you eat much bread? Do you eat a lot of bread?
> How much? How many slices a day?
> I don't eat much bread. I don't eat many slices, perhaps one or two a day. I do eat a lot of crackers, though.

146. *Real* and *sure* are adjectives meaning "genuine" and "certain," respectively. Many native speakers misuse them as adverbs; don't make their mistakes.
Really (and *very*) and *surely* are adverbs meaning "extremely" and "undoubtedly" or "certainly."

> This pocketbook is made of real leather.
> I'm really pleased with the quality of my bag.
> Are you sure they'll be here on time?
> They surely wouldn't want to miss the party.
> I'm very pleased to meet you.

147. The plural of *this* is *these*.
The plural of *that* is *those*. (See also **33;34.**)

> This painting goes well next to these curtains.
> That flower over there is being hidden by those weeds.
> This kind of candy is my favorite; those kinds are not.

POSITION IN SENTENCES

148. Adjectives usually precede the nouns they modify.

> a bright blue sky
> a small flower

They may, however, follow their nouns for special purposes.

> a vision lovely to behold
> something interesting
> the sisters Brontë
> all things wise and wonderful

149. Predicate adjectives follow linking verbs. (See also **56.**)

> Tara is graceful; she also seems healthy and looks beautiful.

150. When the words *first* and *last* modify numbers, place them directly before the numbers.

> The first six weeks of college will be difficult.
> I've been crying for the last 15 minutes.

151. Adjectives of color are usually placed directly before their nouns.

> the old, gray mare
> a sturdy, new, brown table

---

152. In order to avoid confusion, it is usually best to place adverbs as near as possible to the verbs, adjectives, or adverbs that they modify. Take particular care with *almost*, *ever*, *even*, *just*, *hardly*, *not*, and *only*. These five sentences have five different meanings.

> *Only* he said he loved her. (No one else said it.)
> He *only* said he loved her. (He said nothing else.)
> He said *only* he loved her. (No one else loved her.)
> He said he *only* loved her. (Loving her was his sole activity.)
> He said he loved *only* her. (He loved no one else.)

153. When more than one adverb appears in a sentence, the normal order is adverb of manner, frequency, place, and time.

> Paul faithfully waters his plants every day in the den at 9:30 A.M.

154. Place adverbs of time at the beginning of a sentence or at the end.

> Yesterday we went to visit Jorge and Lois.
> They're flying to Puerto Rico tomorrow.

155. Place adverbs of frequency before adverbs of time. Words such as *always*, *frequently*, *never*, *occasionally*, *often*, *seldom*, and *usually* are used in four positions:

> *a.* before main verbs
> *b.* after auxiliary verbs in affirmative statements
> *c.* after the verb *be* in affirmative statements
> *d.* before *be* and auxiliary verbs in short statements or rejoinders

> She frequently grows her own sprouts in the winter.
> He can't always visit his parents when they want him to.
> I am usually swayed by flattery in the morning. You never are.
> Peggy seldom wrote to her aunt when she was young. Prentice always did.
> Toronto is never too hot in the summer. Tulsa always is.

156. Adverbs should not separate verbs from their direct objects.

> *wrong*: I will meet tomorrow the Chinese delegation.
> *right*:   I will meet the Chinese delegation tomorrow.
> *wrong*: Marie sent periodically flowers to her beau.
> *right*:   Marie periodically sent flowers to her beau.

COMPARISONS

Adjectives and adverbs may express a greater or lesser degree of quality or quantity by using the method of comparison (comparative and superlative degrees).

157. The comparative degree is used to compare or relate two items with each other. Most short adjectives and adverbs form this degree by adding *er*. Note the spelling changes in some of these examples.

sharp	sharper	deep	deeper
late	later	white	whiter
lazy	lazier	early	earlier
big	bigger	red	redder

158. The comparative degree of most adjectives and adverbs of more than one syllable is formed by adding *more* or *less*.

difficult	more difficult	often	more often
eager	less eager	slowly	more slowly
efficient	less efficient	frequently	less frequently

159. Never use both the *er* form and the *more/less* form with the same word.

> *wrong*: Scotty was more quieter than Bob.
> *right*: Scotty was quieter than Bob.

160. *Than* usually follows the comparative degree.

> The Daltons were younger than the James brothers.
> August Moon is a less expensive restaurant than Shanghai Palace.
> Guy works harder than his brother.
> She spoke more rapidly than I had anticipated.

However, the following structure is also acceptable:

> He is the wiser of the two brothers.
> Of the two cities, Minneapolis is the larger.

161. The superlative degree is used to compare or relate three or more items with each other. Most short adjectives and adverbs form this degree by adding *est*. Note the spelling changes in some of these examples.

sharp	(the) sharpest	deep	(the) deepest
late	(the) latest	white	(the) whitest
lazy	(the) laziest	early	(the) earliest
big	(the) biggest	red	(the) reddest

162. The superlative degree of most adjectives and adverbs of more than one syllable is formed by adding *most* or *least*.

difficult	(the) most difficult
eager	(the) least eager
efficient	(the) least efficient
often	(the) most often
slowly	(the) most slowly
frequently	(the) least frequently

163. Never use both the *est* form and the *most/least* form with the same word.

> *wrong*: Scotty was the most quietest person in the club.
> *right*:   Scotty was the quietest person in the club.
> *wrong*: Cancer is the most debilitatingest disease imaginable.
> *right*:   Cancer is the most debilitating disease imaginable.

164. The superlative degree of all adjectives and adverbs is preceded by *the*.

> Are the Smiths the youngest of all your clients?
> Wheelers is the least expensive restaurant of the three you mentioned.
> She spoke the most rapidly of all the people on the panel.
> He is the wisest of the three brothers.
> Of the three cities, Northfield is the smallest.

165. Special forms for irregular adjectives and adverbs

Positive	*Comparative*	*Superlative* (with *the*)
bad, badly	worse	worst
far	farther, further	farthest, furthest
good, well	better	best
late	later, latter	latest, last
little	less, lesser	least
many, much, some	more	most

166. Some adjectives and adverbs are absolute; that is, by their definitions, they can't be qualified or compared. If a box is square, then it has equal sides; it is square. It can't be very square. It can't be more square than another box. Square is square.

Degrees of comparison with absolute adjectives and adverbs must use such words as *almost*, *not quite*, or *nearly* to indicate that they are approaching the absolute.

> Of all the coins, this one is the most nearly round. (not the roundest)
> This kitten is almost dead; the other seems fine. (not this kitten is
>   deader than that one)
> The vote in the Senate was not quite unanimous, 99 to 1.

Some examples of absolute terms

absolute	full	single
alone	horizontal	square
blind	indestructable	straight
dead	instantaneous	supreme
empty	perfect	unanimous
equal	pregnant	unique (the only one of
eternal	primary	its kind)
final	right	vertical
first, second, etc.	round	wrong

167. When comparing members of a class, group, or kind, do not compare something to itself.

   a. Use *else* or *other* in the comparative degree.

   > *wrong*: Alaska is larger than any state in the Union. (Alaska is in the Union. It can't be larger than itself. Thus it must somehow be excluded from the rest of the group.)
   > *right*: Alaska is larger than any other state in the Union.
   > Jim's car was faster than any other car in the race.
   > Anne is heavier than anyone else in the laboratory.

   b. Use *all* in the superlative degree.

   > *wrong*: Alaska is the largest state in the Union.
   > *right*: Alaska is the largest of all the states in the Union.
   > His is the fastest of all the cars.
   > She is the heaviest of all the technicians.

168. When using comparisons, take care to see that the sentence has all its ingredients. The omission of *'s* or a word may alter the meaning.

   > *wrong*: The dean's office is larger than the president.
   > (We're not comparing an office to a person, we're comparing an office to an office.)
   > *right*: The dean's office is larger than the president's.
   > *right*: The dean's office is larger than that of the president.

   > *wrong*: Carl loves Chris more than Terry.
   > (Does Carl love Chris more than Terry loves Chris? Or does Carl love Chris more than he loves Terry?)
   > *right*: Carl loves Chris more than Terry does.
   > *right*: Carl loves Chris more than he loves Terry.

169. Note the sentence patterns and structures of these comparison examples.

   > The terrain of Arizona is similar to the terrain of Libya.
   > It is also similar to that of southwestern Peru.
   > Are the climates of the three regions somewhat like each other, too?
   > Yes, the climates are similar to each other.
   > Are the people who live in Arizona the same as the people in the other two places?
   > No, all three groups are different from each other.
   > They're somewhat alike in their need for a good water supply.
   > In all other ways, however, they're rather different from one another.
   > Is Houston as large as Philadelphia?
   > Houston is larger than Philadelphia in size, but Philadelphia is more densely populated.
   > Pennsylvania isn't as large as Texas; Texas is much larger.
   > Atlanta is closer to St. Louis than it is to Denver.
   > Atlanta isn't as close to Denver as it is to St. Louis.

It's farther from New York to San Francisco than it is from Oslo to
   Rome.
It isn't as far from Oslo to Rome as it is from New York to San
   Francisco.
Marin is a better dancer than her sister Maia is.
Marin dances better than Maia does.
Marin is a more skillful dancer than Maia.
Marin dances more skillfully than Maia.
The more Sean wept, the redder his eyes became.
He was sadder than anyone thought.
He wasn't as happy as we believed.

ARTICLES

The three articles *a*, *an*, and *the* are actually limiting adjectives used to modify
nouns.

170. Articles are used with singular countable nouns that have not been
specifically identified. They are used even if a descriptive adjective accompanies the noun.

a telephone	a small, black telephone
an orange	an overly ripe, mandarin orange
the desk	the boss's spacious desk

171. No article is used in the following circumstances:

a. when a determiner specifically identifies the noun

my telephone	Pat's pencil
another orange	Andy's glasses
that desk	one small, black pen

b. when the noun is of indefinite quality or quantity; that is, noncountable (See also **174c**.)

Copper is mined in Zaire.
Ballet is her prime passion.

Note the distinction between countable and noncountable nouns in
these examples:

He has a great support system behind him.
He deserves support from us.

She is the authority in charge of our case.
She can speak with authority on that subject.

c. when the noun is the proper name of a person, street, city, country,
etc., and is not qualified (See also **174b**.)

Ted lives in San Diego at 1250 6th Avenue.
Miriam is going to visit Mount Fuji in Japan.

172. *A* and *an* are indefinite, referring unspecifically to nouns. They are used only with singular nouns.

A is used before words beginning with consonant sounds.

a bird   a historical event
a yellow apron   a university

An is used before words beginning with vowel sounds.

an apricot-colored tie   an hour
an item   an umbrella

173. *The* is definite, referring to a particular noun. It is used with both singular and plural nouns.

the birds   the yellow ties   the universities

174. *The* is also used in the following circumstances:

a. preceding the proper names of rivers, seas, and mountains, and of countries that have been qualified in some way

the Ganges River   the Alps
the Indian Ocean   the Republic of Austria

b. preceding the names of persons, streets, cities, countries, etc., when they are used as proper adjectives (See also **171c.**)

the Korean highlands
the Fourteenth Street merchants
the Stanislovski method of acting
the New York skyline

c. preceding noncountable nouns when the nouns are followed by modifiers (See also **171b.**)

The copper that is mined in Zaire is of high quality.
She loves the ballet of George Balanchine.

Note the distinction between noncountable nouns that have been modified and those that have not in these examples:

Inventiveness was common in his family.
The inventiveness of Jefferson is apparent in his writings.
George is studying sociology.
George is studying the sociology of those strange people.

175. Articles should be repeated in a sentence if the meaning requires it.

The husband and the father came in. (two men)
The husband and father came in. (one man)
She had a red and an orange sweater. (two sweaters)
She had a red and orange sweater. (one sweater)

EXERCISES

(Answers are on pages 131–132.)

A. Circle the word in parentheses that makes the sentence correct.

1. We won't be there (*because, due to*) I have to work late tonight.

2. The kids scarcely (*had, didn't have*) enough money for the movie.

3. The sale was offered (*one time only, one-time-only*).

4. (*Almost, Most*) all my ink is gone.

5. Have you seen today's paper (*already, yet*)?

6. I don't have (*any, some*) faith in that solution.

7. Is Ahmad (*anymore, still*) dating Jasmine?

8. Albert took the idea of time relativity (*farther, further*) than anyone dreamed he could.

9. I've had (*fewer, less*) trouble remembering names since I took that memory course.

10. You ski (*good, well*). How long have you been taking lessons?

11. We eat (*a lot of, many*) peanut butter in our house.

12. I don't think I like (*that, those*) brand of shoes.

13. (*Only I, I only*) had two pieces of chocolate, I assure you.

14. Amanda (*occasionally is, is occasionally*) temperamental.

15. Hassan is (*a more elegant, an eleganter*) dresser than his brother.

16. San Antonio was larger (*as, than*) I had expected.

17. That's the (*most clean, cleanest*) I've ever seen your refrigerator.

18. Your hypothetical equation is (*more, more nearly*) perfect than any other I've seen.

19. Is Jakarta (*as, so*) large as Singapore?

20. Pietr can skate (*better, as well*) than his friend Helga.

21. (*The genius, Genius*) is 1 percent inspiration and 99 percent perspiration.

22. It was truly (*a, an*) historical moment.

23. The psychic phenomenon he spoke of is called (*the Kirlian, Kirlian*) effect.

24. I've decided which one I want. I want the black and (*the white, white*) set.

B. In each of the following pairs of sentences, one sentence is grammatically correct, while the other is not. Write the letter of the correct sentence in the space provided.

Example: ___b___ (*a*) He isn't not here.
(*b*) He isn't here.

1. _____ (*a*) She missed the performance due to her running out of gas.
(*b*) She missed the performance because she ran out of gas.

2. _____ (*a*) This is the year when she starts the sixth grade.
(*b*) This is the year that she starts the sixth grade.

3. _____ (*a*) These woods are lovely dark and deep.
(*b*) The performers were young, vivacious, and talented.

4. _____ (*a*) Is that a turn-of-the-century vase you just bought?
(*b*) We'll try to teach them some self respect.

5. _____ (*a*) Do you have to be twenty one to buy beer in that state?
(*b*) Do you have to be twenty-one to buy beer in that state?

6. _____ (*a*) She's been living here for the last ten years.
(*b*) The three first people in the race will all get trophies.

7. _____ (a) Christopher's fans were waiting to see him last night.

    (b) We're going tomorrow to see *Othello* at the Warner Theater.

8. _____ (a) Her absence was due to the fact that her car broke down.

    (b) She was late due to the fact that her car broke down.

9. _____ (a) Reno is the city where many people get divorced.

    (b) They went where they could get an easy divorce.

10. _____ (a) Merlin seldom doesn't use dental floss.

    (b) Dr. Holden seldom misses an opportunity to play golf.

11. _____ (a) My desk has a large, attractive, ceramic pen holder.

    (b) Your portable gray electric typewriter works well, doesn't it?

12. _____ (a) Her small blue flight bag cost $19.95.

    (b) The white small bottle of polish cost $1.98.

13. _____ (a) Only we needed a few more minutes to finish.

    (b) We needed only a few more minutes to finish.

14. _____ (a) Mr. Smith methodically tunes up his car once a month, usually in his garage on a Saturday morning.

    (b) Susan daily, normally, carefully, after she uses them, cleans her wood-working tools.

15. _____ (a) She threatened never to speak to him again.

    (b) I've never seen nothing like it.

16. _____ (a) Hope always was more happier than her brother.

    (b) Mrs. Kowalski is quieter than she used to be.

17. _____ (a) This is the most amazing glue I've ever used.

    (b) We walked in the least deepest parts of the river.

18. _____ (a) We're not quite alone yet; my brother is still here.

(b) That's one of the most unique tricks I've ever seen in a magic show.

19. _____ (a) Our house is larger than any other on our street.

(b) Jesse ran faster than anyone today.

20. _____ (a) Claude is the best chess player in his club.

(b) This is the worst of all the colds I've ever had.

C. Circle the adjective or the adverb in parentheses that makes the sentence correct.

1. This candy tastes too (*sweet, sweetly*) for me.

2. They told me the broth was hot, so I tasted it (*careful, carefully*).

3. We tried your theory, and it proved (*false, falsely*).

4. Ms. Brown lives (*fair, fairly*) close to her mother-in-law.

5. That politician has a (*high, highly*) opinion of himself.

6. Frankly, I think his reputation is (*high, highly*) overrated.

7. The pitcher threw the ball (*high, highly*) and away from the batter.

8. Your problem seems (*bad, badly*).

9. The more he chased her, the more (*quick, quickly*) she ran.

10. Those gardenias smell (*wonderful, wonderfully*).

11. I can tell that this meal is going to be (*delicious, deliciously*).

12. You look tired. Do you feel (*healthy, healthily*)?

13. Your machine types (*noisy, noisily*).

14. Your football coach says that you are really (*good, well*) at the sport.

15. The situation has become (*worse, badly*) than before.

D. Write the appropriate form of the adjective or adverb in each of the following sentences.

Example: (*big*) Which of these four is the _____ biggest? _____

1. (*invitingly*) This bouquet is arranged _____

   _____ than that one.

2. (*interesting*) Vancouver is _____ of

   all the Canadian cities we visted.

3. (*well*) I feel much _____ now that

   I've rested.

4. (*straight*) Of all these lines, which do you think is _____

   _____ ?

5. (*late*) It's quite late; indeed, it's probably _____

   _____ than you realize.

6. (*some*) Do you think Bess wrote _____

   letters than Harry did?

7. (*long*) I think this string is _____

   that one.

8. (*meek*) Princess was the _____ of all

   the kittens in the litter.

9. (*cuddly*) She was also the _____ of

   all of them.

10. (*clear*) Your TV picture seems _____

    mine.

E. Fill in the missing forms of the adjectives and adverbs in the table below.

	POSITIVE	COMPARATIVE	SUPERLATIVE
1.	sad		
2.		bluer	
3.			worst
4.			most difficult
5.		more interesting	
6.	capable		
7.	early		
8.		nearer	
9.			farthest
10.			least forcefully
11.		less dramatically	
12.	loudly		

F. Circle the word in parentheses that makes the sentence correct.

1. They gave us (*less, fewer*) food than we had ordered.

2. My mother always likes to buy (*that, those*) brand of cigarettes.

3. The union leader said he couldn't compromise any (*farther, further*) than he already had.

4. The bill that Senator Kennedy introduced sounded (*good, well*) to us.

5. The poll showed that (*almost, most*) people pay their taxes.

6. Hearing that news gives me (*real, really*) satisfaction.

7. Convinced that she was right, Cybil said, "(*Sure, Surely*), you are mistaken."

8. I have (*already, yet*) taken that course.

9. Mr. Kuykendahl said he didn't have (*any, some*) interest in our project.

10. Yes, she's (*anymore, still*) a fan of bullfighting.

11. Have you learned (*many, much*) English this year?

12. The only (*sure, surely*) way to find out is to ask.

13. I'm (*real, really*) glad to meet you.

14. (*Almost, Most*) anyone can learn to crochet.

15. Anyone who eats and exercises (*good, well*) will certainly look (*good, well*).

16. Dave Jennings can kick a football (*farther, further*) than I can.

17. I'm not sure whether I should get (*this, these*) curtains or those.

18. They gave us (*less, fewer*) bags of food than we had ordered.

19. How (*many, much*) bags did you order?

20. I don't know why they sent it there, I'm not living on Bradley Boulevard (*anymore, still*).

21. I can get you (*any, some*) new ones, if you'd like.

22. I can't believe it; you haven't seen their new home (*already, yet*)?

G. Some of the following sentences contain errors in grammar, structure, or usage. If the sentence is correct, circle the letter *C* (for correct). If the sentence contains an error, underline the error and circle the letter *I* (for incorrect). Then rewrite the sentence correctly in the spaces provided.

Example: Nobuo is <u>fastest</u> than Chen.   C Ⓘ
Nobuo is faster than Chen.

1. Mieko's peaches are as juicy as Alvin.   C I

_____

_____

2. The faster I go, the behinder I get.   C   I

_____

_____

3. Those students are similar from each other.   C   I

_____

_____

4. The more Bonita shouted, the quieter Joan became.   C   I

_____

_____

5. There aren't as many apples in my basket as there are
   oranges in yours.   C   I

_____

_____

6. Your daughters seem quite different from each other.   C   I

_____

_____

7. Carrie is closer to her mother than she is to her father. C   I

_____

_____

8. Are the people in southern Algeria the same like the
   people in the north?   C   I

_____

_____

9. Jackson is a most skilled player than Dent.   C   I

_____

_____

10. It wasn't as cold as we had thought.   C   I

_____

_____

H. Complete each of the following sentences by writing in *a* or *an*; write an *X* if no article is required.

This past summer we bought _____ camper. _____ camper is like
                                      1   2

_____ small bus, but it is more comfortable than _____ bus.
   3   4

Ours has _____ icebox, _____ table, and _____ area that we use
             5   6   7

for _____ storage. Our _____ sleeping space is big enough for
      8   9

_____ ten people. _____ added advantage in _____ this camper
   10   11   12

is that it uses _____ regular gasoline. We like to eat _____ fruit
                   13   14

in the morning for _____ breakfast, so we always keep _____
                       15   16

supply of _____ apples and _____ oranges in one of the cabinets.
              17   18

One _____ day we even bought _____ watermelon.
       19   20

I. Complete each of the following sentences by writing in the article *the* if it is required or by writing an *X* if it is not.

1. _____ madness of Rasputin is well documented.

2. _____ fire has been called humanity's greatest discovery.

3. I hear that _____ price of gold has gone up again.

4. _____ seafood is very good at this restaurant.

5. Our mayor spoke to us about _____ crime problem in the city.

6. An acronym for _____ Great Lakes is HOMES.

7. Our Constitution guarantees the right to _____ life.

8. _____ Mexican border with the U.S. is long.

9. _____ milk is our favorite beverage.

10. _____ beer you're drinking is made in Milwaukee.

11. Both the President and _____ Vice President are Westerners.

12. The blue and _____ green rug in the hallway needs cleaning.

ANSWER KEY

The number in parentheses after an answer refers to the rule in this section that covers this point.

A.
1. because (**131**)
2. had (**132b**)
3. one time only (**137**)
4. Almost (**138**)
5. yet (**139**)
6. any (**140**)
7. still (**141**)
8. further (**142**)
9. less (**143**)
10. well (**144**)
11. a lot of (**145**)
12. that (**147**)
13. I only (**152**)
14. is occasionally (**155c**)
15. a more elegant (**158**)
16. than (**160**)
17. cleanest (**161**)
18. more nearly (**166**)
19. as (**169**)
20. better (**169**)
21. Genius (**171b**)
22. a (**172**)
23. the Kirlian (**174b**)
24. white (**175**)

B.
1. *b* (**131**)
2. *b* (**133**)
3. *b* (**136**)
4. *a* (**137**)
5. *b* (**137**)
6. *a* (**150**)
7. *a* (**154**)
8. *a* (**131**)
9. *b* (**133**)
10. *b* (**132b**)
11. *a* (**136**)
12. *a* (**151**)
13. *b* (**152**)
14. *a* (**153**)
15. *a* (**132b**)
16. *b* (**159**)
17. *a* (**163**)
18. *a* (**166**)
19. *a* (**167a**)
20. *b* (**167b**)

C. All of the answers in this exercise refer to rule **149** and the uses of adverbs and adjectives in general.

1. sweet
2. carefully
3. false
4. fairly
5. high
6. highly
7. high
8. bad
9. quickly
10. wonderful
11. delicious
12. healthy
13. noisily
14. good
15. worse

D.
1. more invitingly (**158**)
2. the most interesting (**162; 164**)
3. better (**165**)
4. the most nearly straight (**166**)
5. later (**157**)
6. more (**165**)
7. longer than (**160**)
8. meekest (**161**)
9. most cuddly (**162**)
10. clearer than (**160**)

E. All of the answers in this exercise refer to sections **157–169**.

Positive	Comparative	Superlative
1. sad	sadder	saddest
2. blue	bluer	bluest
3. bad, badly	worse	worst
4. difficult	more difficult	most difficult
5. interesting	more interesting	most interesting
6. capable	more/less capable	most/least capable
7. early	earlier	earliest
8. near	nearer	nearest
9. far	farther	farthest
10. forcefully	less forcefully	least forcefully
11. dramatically	less dramatically	least dramatically
12. loudly	more/less loudly	most/least loudly

F.

1. less (143)	12. sure (146)
2. that (147)	13. really (146)
3. further (142)	14. Almost (138)
4. good (144)	15. well; good (144)
5. most (138)	16. farther (142)
6. real (146)	17. these (147)
7. Surely (146)	18. fewer (143)
8. already (139)	19. many (145)
9. any (140)	20. anymore (141)
10. still (141)	21. some (140)
11. much (145)	22. yet (139)

G.

underline	circle	underline	circle
1. Alvin	I (168)	6.	C (169)
2. behinder	I (158)	7.	C (169)
3. from	I (169)	8. like	I (169)
4.	C (169)	9. most	I (169)
5.	C (169)	10.	C (169)

Example: Nobuo is faster than Chen.

1. Mieko's peaches are as juicy as Alvin's.
2. The faster I go, the more behind I get.
3. Those students are similar to each other.
8. Are the people in southern Algeria the same as the people in the north?
9. Jackson is a more skilled player than Dent.

H. All of the answers in this exercise refer to rules **170–172.**

1. a	8. X	15. X
2. A	9. X	16. a
3. a	10. X	17. X
4. a	11. An	18. X
5. an	12. X	19. X
6. a	13. X	20. a
7. an	14. X	

I.

1. The (174*c*)	7. X (171*b*)
2. X (174*c*)	8. The (174*b*)
3. the (170; 173)	9. X (171*b*)
4. The (170; 173)	10. The (174*c*)
5. the (170; 173)	11. the (175)
6. the (170; 173)	12. X (175)

Prepositions

176. Since prepositions require objects, be sure that all pronouns that are objects of prepositions are in the objective case. (See also **43c**.)

wrong: He was asked to choose between Jack and I.
right: He was asked to choose between Jack and me.

Are you coming with her and me?
Don't be afraid of him or her.

177. Repeat prepositions if clarity requires it.

wrong: Prince Edward thought more of his dog than his son.
(Did he think more of his dog than he thought of his son? Or did he think more of his dog than his son thought of the dog?)
right: Prince Edward thought more of his dog than of his son.

wrong: She looks better in green than brown.
(This construction could actually mean that she looks better in green than brown looks in green.)
right: She looks better in green than in brown.

178. Take care not to repeat or use prepositions needlessly.

wrong: Of what are you afraid of?
right: Of what are you afraid?
right: What are you afraid of?

wrong: The racehorse wandered off of the track.
right: The racehorse wandered off the track.

179. Many people think that prepositions should not be used to end sentences. This is not true. While it is true that most sentences can be strengthened by ending them with some other part of speech, there is nothing grammatically wrong with these constructions.

What is your aunt looking for?
I'm not sure I know what you're talking about.
That's not the sort of behavior that I'm going to put up with.

SPECIAL USAGE NOTES

180. *Among* is used to compare three or more items.

Let's keep the news secret among the three of us.
I knew I'd be among friends at Sam's party.

Between is used to compare two items.

> Nothing has ever come between her husband and her.
> There is little difference between the two candidates.

181. *As* is a conjunction expressing similarity and comparing verbs. It is also a preposition meaning "in the capacity of" or "in the role of."
Like is a preposition meaning "similar to."
Like and *as* may not be used interchangeably. Note the construction in these examples.

> That cloud looks like a duck. (*preposition*)
> You are just like your mother. (*preposition*)
> Grandpa doesn't see as well as he used to. (*conjunction*)
> You should do as you are told. (*conjunction*)
> He works part-time as a bookkeeper. (*preposition*)

182. *As far as* (and *to*) are used with expressions of distance.
Until is used with expressions of time, direct or implied.

> I'll wait for you until five o'clock.
> I couldn't wait until she got home; I had to leave.
> Until next time. (a parting expression)
> I'll walk as far as the corner.
> I'll walk to the corner.
> Is Stephens City as far as Winchester from here?

Until is often contracted as *'til*.

> 'til then.   Wait 'til tomorrow.

183. *Beside* is a preposition meaning "next to."
Besides is an adverb meaning "in addition to."

> I sat beside your uncle at dinner last night.
> Did you park your car beside mine?
> What do you want to serve for dinner besides the chicken and rice?
> Besides typing, I'm also taking shorthand in school this year.

184. *Despite* and *in spite of* may be used interchangeably when followed by a noun.

> Despite his age, he worked as hard as his grandson.
> In spite of his age, he worked as hard as his grandson.

When these terms are followed by a clause, they must change to *despite the fact that* and *in spite of the fact that*.

> Despite the fact that we had lost, we were in good spirits.
> In spite of the fact that we had lost, we were in good spirits.

185. *Differ from* means "to be dissimilar."
Differ with means "to disagree."

> Your car differs from mine.
> Lily differs from her sister in looks and in temperament.
> Fred differs with me on this matter.
> I differ with your opinion, but I'm still your friend.

186. *Different from* is a phrase used in a comparison. It means "to be unlike." Never use *than* after *different. Than* is a conjunction, not a preposition or part of a verb.

> *wrong:* Life here is no different than life anywhere else.
> *right:* Life here is no different from life anywhere else.

> Her approach is different from any we've seen before.
> I see that you dress quite differently from the way your brother does.

187. *During* answers the question *when.*

> When will you visit Tommy and Kevin? I'll try to drop in on them during the next few weeks.
> When did Betsy come back? She arrived during our lunch break.

188. *For* shows the length of time of an action.

> Leonid has worked here for four months.
> My family has been living in this valley for 150 years.

Since shows the time the action began.

> Leonid has worked here since March.
> My family has been living in this valley since the middle of the nineteenth century.

189. *In* means "within"; it expresses no action.
Into means "from outside to within," expressing the action of movement.

> She dived into the pool. Once she was in the pool, she didn't want to come out.
> Gina put her key into the lock, opened the door, and walked into the house. Bill was already there, in the kitchen.

190. *In, on, at, by, with*

> ***a.*** A person travels *on* a plane, train, boat, or bus; but a person travels *in* a car or taxi.

> > Do you usually come to work *on* a bus?
> > No, I usually ride *in* my neighbor's car.

b. A person travels *by* car, taxi, plane, train, boat, etc.

> Did you come to work *by* car today?
> I love traveling *by* steamship.

c. One who walks or rides a horse might use *on* in these constructions:

> I usually come in a car or by cab, but today I came *on* foot.
> Tomorrow I plan to arrive *on* horseback.

d. *With* means "accompanying" or "as a companion of."
By, when used with a reflexive pronoun, means "alone" or "unaccompanied." (See also **27**.)

> Did your sister-in-law go *with* you to the hospital?
> No, I went *by* myself.
> At lunch, she usually sits *by* herself, not *with* her friends.

e. *With* refers to an instrument; *in* refers to the substance of the instrument.

> Did you sign your check *with* a pencil?
> I think you should sign *with* a pen.
> Banks usually like signatures *in* ink, don't they?

f. When referring to an address, note that one lives

at a specific address	at 4740 Booker St.
on a specific street	on Booker Street
in a specific city, state, country	in Chapel Hill
	in North Carolina
	in the U.S.

g. When referring to times and dates, note that a person is born

at a specific time	at 12 noon
on a specific day	on Tuesday
	on January 28, 1969
in a specific month	in January
in a specific year	in 1969
in a specific city	in Washington, D.C.

The above person is said to be *from* Washington.

191. Many words add prepositions for emphasis. For example, *hurry up* seems stronger than just *hurry*. If something is said to be *dried out*, it is completely *dried*. There are, however, many words that call for a particular preposition in order to express a certain meaning. Here is a partial list of such words with their prepositions and meanings.

abide by: accept the consequences of

abstain from: refrain from by one's own choice

according to: on the authority of

agree to: be in accord with something

agree with: be of the same opinion as another person

back down: retreat from a position
bear up under: endure
break in, into, in on: interrupt
bring about: cause to happen

call off: cancel
calm down: become calm or undisturbed
capable of: having sufficient resources
carry on: continue
catch on: understand
clean out: clean the inside of
clear up: clarify
come about: happen
come across: find accidentally
come back: return
come from: be born in or originate in
come out: appear, be published; develop; finish
complementary to: completing
conversant with: well informed about
count on: depend upon
cross out: cancel

deal in: do business in, sell, trade
die down: subside, become quiet
do away with: abolish, discontinue
do over: repeat; redecorate
draw near: approach
dress up: put on one's finest clothing
drive at: hint, mean
drop out: cease to attend
drown out: overwhelm and blur by a louder sound

eat away: gradually consume
edge out: win a contest by a slight margin
egg on: incite

face up to: meet or confront
fall for: become infatuated with; be naive about
farm out: delegate a job to another
fed up with: out of patience or bored
feel up to: be capable of
find out: discover
follow through: carry out to completion
fresh from: recently returned

get back at: gain revenge
get over: recover
give in: surrender
go into: discuss
go off: explode
go out: stop burning or producing light
grow up: reach maturity

hands down: conclusively
have (it) in for: hold a grudge against
head off: intercept
hear from: receive a message
hold out: delay; refuse to concede
hold over: retain longer than planned
hold up: rob

interfere in: hinder or impede something
interfere with: hinder or impede someone

jump at: grab or accept eagerly

keep at, on: continue, persist
keep to (the right, the left, etc.): bear toward (the direction)
keep up: maintain
knock out: render unconscious

labor under: suffer from

lay off: dismiss workers during a slack period

let go of: release one's grasp

live up to: match or equal a standard set by another

look down on: consider inferior

look into, over: investigate, examine

look up to: admire, respect

make of: understand, interpret

make out: succeed; distinguish

make up: constitute; invent; reconcile; apply cosmetics

make up for: compensate, atone

name after, for: give the same name as

number among: include in a group

own up: confess

pan out: result

pass away: die

pass for: be considered as

pass up: forgo, reject

pick on: tease, nag, annoy

pick up: lift; improve; offer a ride

play along with: cooperate temporarily

pop in: visit unexpectedly

pore over: study carefully

pull out: retreat, withdraw; leave

put down: lay aside; suppress; humiliate

put off: postpone

put (one) up: supply a place to sleep (for someone)

put up with: tolerate

read up on: study carefully

reel off: recite quickly

ring up: call by telephone

round off: express a number approximately

round up: capture, gather, herd together

rub (it) in: remind someone repeatedly of a mistake

rub out: erase

run across, into: meet or find unexpectedly

run away: leave home; escape

run out of: exhaust one's supply

run out on: abandon, foresake

run over: hit with an automobile

salt away: save, store up

see (one) off: say goodbye to someone at the starting point of a trip

see through: understand the true or hidden nature of

set up: begin; put together

settle down: adopt a regular lifestyle

settle on: agree

sew up: conclude

shake-up: a reorganization or change

show off: attract attention in a vivid way

shut up: stop talking

side with: favor, align oneself with

single out: choose one from among many

size up: estimate the value of

slip up: miscalculate, make a mistake

snow under: overburden

sound out: test; get views indirectly

square off: prepare for battle by confronting the opposition

stack up: compare

stand in for: take someone's place, substitute

stand out: be prominent

stand up: fail to appear for an appointment

stand up for: defend, side with

step up: increase

stick up: rob

stir up: incite, provoke

strike up: start playing

swear in: induct into office by oath
swear off: give up

take after: resemble
take for: consider mistakenly
take off: remove; depart; deduct
take up with: consult
talk into: persuade
talk over: discuss
thanks to: because of
think up: invent, devise
throw up: vomit
tide over: help through a difficult period
tie up: engage busily
time off: period when one doesn't work
touch off: ignite, cause to explode
touch up: make minor improvements or changes
tune in: adjust a radio or TV to receive signals
turn down: reject
turn in: hand in or give over; go to bed
turn out: result, end up, develop; produce

turn up: appear

uncalled for: tactless, impolite
up to: dependent upon one's decision; physically capable

wait on: serve
warm up (to): become more friendly (with someone)
washed up: finished, failed
watered down: diluted, weakened
wear out: become unusable through heavy use
weed out: select the best and discard the worst
what with: considering
what's up?: what's happening?
win over: convert someone to one's point of view
write-up: an account of a person or an event

year in and year out (also for days, weeks, months): regularly, over a long period

EXERCISES
(Answers are on page 144.)

A. Circle the word or words in parentheses that make the sentence correct.

1. Phila gave the present to my wife and (*I, me*).

2. She sleeps better in her own bed than (*her neighbor's, in her neighbor's*).

3. The child fell (*off of, off*) the swing.

4. I hope we can keep this information just (*between, among*) the two of us.

5. Constantin's mother told him to act (*as, like*) a gentleman.

6. Hans is only traveling with us (*until, as far as*) Stockholm.

7. (*Beside, Besides*) the laundry, do you also want me to do the dishes?

8. He asked to have Pierre on his team (*in spite of, in spite of the fact that*) they hadn't spoken in years.

9. Your version differs (*from, with*) mine in two key areas.

10. The band's new uniforms are quite different (*from, than*) the old ones, aren't they?

11. (*During, When*) my stay in Belgium, I visited my old friend, Matthieu.

12. Gad has been working in that restaurant (*for, since*) six years.

13. The doe ran (*in, into*) the forest and disappeared.

14. Peg was born (*at, in, on*) March 7, 1910.

15. I plan to go to Cincinnati (*by, in*) train.

16. I'm not eating (*by, with*) myself today; I'm having lunch with Bill Leighton.

17. Mustafa lives (*at, on, in*) Langford Road.

18. It took me a while to catch (*on, by*), but now I understand.

19. He said he was fresh (*by, from*) law school.

20. Conductor, we're ready; strike (*out, up*) the band.

B. Circle the word or words in parentheses that make the sentence correct.

1. There's not much to choose (*between, among*) this year's large field of candidates.

2. All is (*as, like*) it should be.

3. I won't be able to wait (*as far as, until*) my birthday to open the presents; I'm too excited.

4. There's your book, over there (*beside, besides*) Ndala's.

5. Somehow, (*despite, despite the fact that*) wind and rain, the mail got delivered.

6. The speaker differed (*from, with*) the President on the plan to cut back on social programs.

7. I haven't had a good night's sleep (*for, since*) last Thursday.

8. The bread is already (*in, into*) the toaster.

9. The number of people who ride (*on, in*) trains has increased yearly.

10. Mr. Flores did his last painting (*in, by*) watercolors.

11. Allard's best friend is (*of, from*) Namibia.

12. I'll meet you (*at, on*) 5:15 today.

C. Each of the sentences below contains a blank space indicating that a preposition has been left out. Choose the preposition from the list below that best completes each sentence and write it in the blank.

across	by	into	over
after	down on	off	to
at	for	on	up
away	in	out	with

1. It's late. I think I'll turn _____ for the night.

2. They agreed _____ our conditions.

3. Will you clear _____ that point for me; I didn't understand it.

4. Carlos came _____ an old photo of his grandfather in the back of the drawer.

5. How did those photos you took come _____ ?

6. Are you going to do your living room _____ in a Victorian style?

7. I hope she gets _____ her illness in time for her trip.

8. The firecrackers went _____ at nine o'clock, as scheduled.

9. Is it true that the National Bank was held _____ yesterday?

10. Professor Dexter asked us not to interfere _____ him.

11. Have you been keeping _____ your chess-playing skills?

12. The queen looked _____ her subjects as though they were less than human.

13. I was named _____ my great-grandfather.

14. Did your cousin pass _____ because of a heart attack?

15. We offered to pick _____ the hitchhiker.

16. The Army was forced to pull _____, leaving a gap in the defense.

17. We have enough room to put _____ four extra people tonight.

18. The police rounded the thieves _____ after a long chase.

19. I know I'm wrong; don't keep rubbing it _____.

20. That child has a history of running _____ from home.

21. Don't cross in the middle; you might get run _____ by a truck.

22. I don't know when Harold will be here; he often shows _____ late.

23. Jacob can't attend the meeting. Will you stand _____ for him, please?

24. After having too much to drink, Jerry swore _____ liquor forever.

25. Gino has been trying to talk me _____ going to Spain with his group.

26. The new tax law touched _____ a large demonstration.

27. Be sure to tune _____ next week to this same station.

28. It looks as though you're wearing _____ your shoes; the soles have holes in them already.

29. That remark was insulting and totally uncalled _____ .

D. For each of the words on the left, find its definition on the right. Then write the letter of the word in the blank.

a.	rob	1. _____	call off
b.	compare	2. _____	draw near
c.	serve	3. _____	egg on
d.	admire	4. _____	hold up
e.	recover from	5. _____	pass away
f.	incite	6. _____	put off
g.	considering	7. _____	stack up
h.	cancel	8. _____	talk into
i.	hint	9. _____	wait on
j.	endure	10. _____	what with
k.	die	11. _____	look up to
l.	approach	12. _____	own up
m.	confess	13. _____	get over
n.	persuade	14. _____	drive at
o.	postpone	15. _____	bear up under

ANSWER KEY

The number in parentheses after an answer refers to the rule in this section that covers this point.

A.
1. me (**176**)
2. in her neighbor's (**177**)
3. off (**178**)
4. between (**180**)
5. like (**181**)
6. as far as (**182**)
7. Besides (**183**)
8. in spite of the fact that (**184**)
9. from (**185**)
10. from (**186**)

11. During (**187**)
12. for (**188**)
13. into (**189**)
14. on (**190g**)
15. by (**190b**)
16. by (**190d**)
17. on (**190f**)
18. on (**191**)
19. from (**191**)
20. up (**191**)

B.
1. among (**180**)
2. as (**181**)
3. until (**182**)
4. beside (**183**)
5. despite (**184**)
6. with (**185**)

7. since (**188**)
8. in (**189**)
9. on (**190a**)
10. in (**190e**)
11. from (**190g**)
12. at (**190g**)

C. All of the answers in this exercise refer to rule **191**.

1. in
2. to
3. up
4. across
5. out
6. over
7. over
8. off

9. up
10. with
11. up
12. down on
13. after/for
14. away
15. up
16. out

17. up
18. up
19. in
20. away
21. over
22. up
23. in
24. off

25. into
26. off
27. in
28. out
29. for

D. All of the answers in this exercise refer to rule **191**.

1. *h*
2. *l*
3. *f*
4. *a*
5. *k*

6. *o*
7. *b*
8. *n*
9. *c*
10. *g*

11. *d*
12. *m*
13. *e*
14. *i*
15. *j*

Conjunctions, Interjections, Expletives, and Appositives

192. *After, before*, and *but* may be used both as conjunctions and as prepositions. The case of the pronoun that follows one of these words depends on the word's use.

> Dante arrived after me. (*preposition*)
> Dante arrived after I had already left. (*conjunction*)
> Gail dived into the pool before me. (*preposition*)
> Gail dived into the pool before I did. (*conjunction*)
> Everyone will be there but her. (*preposition*)
> Everyone will be there, but she has to stay home. (*conjunction*)

193. The following words are not conjunctions; thus, they may not be used to introduce clauses.

> *like* (a preposition or a verb)
> *providing* (a verb form)
> *the reason is because* (an incorrect phrase; the correct phrase is "the reason is that")
> *without* (a preposition)

> Wilbert insisted that his daughter write as he does. (not "like he does")
> Luigi will be here provided he can remember the address.
> The reason I was unable to wash the clothes was that we ran out of soap.

194. Conjunctive or transitional adverbs are adverbs that are used as conjunctions; that is, they join two independent clauses. In addition, they modify the clauses that they introduce.

> The two sides met again today; *however*, they reached no settlement.
> Rex is moving to Albuquerque; *thus*, we must find a new assistant.
> You promised that our flowers would be ready; *in fact*, you said they'd be boxed and shipped today.

Notice that the conjunctive adverbs are preceded by semicolons and followed by commas. Here is a list of the most common conjunctive and transitional adverbs:

accordingly	hence	in other words	on the contrary
also	however	instead	on the other hand
anyway	in addition	likewise	or else
besides	incidentally	meanwhile	otherwise
consequently	indeed	moreover	still
for example	in fact	nevertheless	therefore
furthermore			thus

195. Subordinate conjunctions join dependent clauses to main or independent clauses. When the dependent clause comes first in a sentence, it is usually followed by a comma. Note that in the last example the dependent clause follows the independent clause.

> Unless you register, you cannot attend classes.
> After I bake cookies, I'll vacuum the floor.
> We're going to proceed although we may end early.

Here is a list of the most common subordinate conjunctions:

after	before	since	until
although	even though	than	when
as	if	that	where
as if	in order that	though	whether
because	lest	unless	while

196. Coordinate conjunctions are used to connect items of equal rank. They may connect words, phrases, or clauses. When they connect independent clauses of four or more words in a compound sentence, they are preceded by commas.

> Bruce *and* Liane swam *and* rode.
> The ball went out the window *but* not through the fence.
> His shoes were made of three different-colored suedes, *yet* oddly enough, they were attractive.

The most common coordinate conjunctions:

and	but	or
yet	for (meaning "because")	nor

197. Correlative conjunctions are used to connect items of the same kind. They are used in pairs. Do not confuse or mix up these pairs; use them as they are listed.

as . . . as	either . . . or
neither . . . nor	not only . . . but also
so . . . as	whether . . . or
both . . . and	if . . . then

Gibson is as tall as his uncle.
The meal was not only good, but also cheap.
The bus driver explained that if we couldn't pay, then we couldn't ride.

198. Correlative conjunctions should be used to correlate (connect) two elements. If more than two elements are involved, a correlative is inappropriate.

> *wrong*: Neither Mary, Meg, nor Martha will accompany you.
> *right*: You will not be accompanied by Mary, or by Meg, or by Martha.

199. When using coordinate or correlative conjunctions, take care that the items joined are of equal rank and are parallel or of similar form. The best way to ensure this is to place the conjunction as near as possible to the item it connects.

> *wrong*: She both gave me money and food.
> *right*: She gave me both money and food.
> (The first sentence is wrong because *both . . . and* is used to join a verb and a noun.)

> *wrong*: We neither have the time nor the money to go to the opera.
> *right*: We have neither the time nor the money to go to the opera.

> We want you not only to see the exhibit but also to taste the food.
> He said he didn't care whether we walked or rode.

200. Most appositives are nonrestrictive phrases in sentences. As such, they need to be set off from their nouns or pronouns and the rest of the sentence by commas.

> Helen Chones, an elequent speaker, led off the program.
> Marie Curie, a brilliant scientist, was awarded two Nobel prizes.

201. When pronouns are used as appositives (in apposition), they must agree with their nouns or pronouns in number and case. (See also 44.)

> The director has asked for two volunteers, you and me.

(*Volunteers* is the object of the verb; thus, the words in apposition to *volunteers* must also be in the objective case.)

> We girls are going out shopping now.

(*Girls* is the subject of the sentence, so the pronoun in apposition to *girls* must also be in the nominative case.)

202. *There, here*, and *it*, when used as expletives, help to provide emphasis or smoothness in sentences. An expletive is never the subject of a sentence. The subject is always the predicate nominative. The verb, therefore, must agree with the predicate nominative.

> There is a mosquito in the room. (*Mosquito* is the subject.)
> It was I who called you yesterday. (*I* is the subject.)
> There are 23 players on the team. (*Players* is the subject.)
> Here come the Smiths. (*Smiths* is the subject.)

203. Interjections have no grammatical relationship to any other words in sentences. They are usually punctuated with exclamation points. Some words are pure interjections, but almost any word can be used as an interjection.

Wow! You made a hole-in-one!
Klaus! I can't believe it's really you!

EXERCISE

Circle the word or words in parentheses that make the sentence correct.

1. Gilda signed up for the course before (*I, me*).
2. Vanessa promised to do the job (*providing, provided*) she could work at home.
3. The Delgado family is moving (*, consequently/; consequently*), we'll have new neighbors within a month.
4. The committee said it would neither accept (*or, nor*) reject the proposal; it would compromise.
5. After the workout, Brett (*was both, both was*) tired and sore.
6. The people on the train will be the Schwartzes, the Raabs, and (*we, us*), the Kamals.
7. You may use the telephone after (*I, me*) finish talking to Theo.
8. When she asked me why we weren't flying, I replied that (*the reason was because, the reason was that*) we preferred trains.
9. The firewood was not only dry (*but, but also*) well aged; it burned well.
10. They're going to (*either go, go either*) to Jamaica or to Aruba on their vacation.

ANSWER KEY

The number in parentheses after the answer refers to the rule in this section that covers this point.

1. me (**192**)
2. provided (**193**)
3. ; consequently (**194**)
4. nor (**197**)
5. was both (**199**)

6. we (**201; 41***b*)
7. I (**192**)
8. the reason was that (**193**)
9. but also (**197**)
10. go either (**199**)

The Sentence

SENTENCE SENSE

204. A sentence needs a subject and a predicate (verb). The subject tells whom or what we are talking about, and the predicate tells what the subject does. This is true in both affirmative and negative statements and in questions. In imperative mood sentences, the subject is often implied but not stated. (See also **58**.)

> Clare sings.
> Blanche doesn't sing.
> Does Ralph sing?
> Stand up. (*You* is the understood subject.)

205. Do not mistake phrases for sentences.

> *wrong*: After coming in from the rain. The dog shook water all over the floor.
> (The first part is a phrase or fragment, not a sentence; it has no predicate.)
> *right*: After she came in from the rain, the dog shook water all over the floor.

> *wrong*: Marybeth. Swimming at top speed.
> (The first part has no predicate; the second part is a participial phrase or fragment that should modify the subject.)
> *right*: Marybeth, swimming at top speed, won the race.

206. Do not mistake dependent clauses for sentences.

> *wrong*: Vadim was about to drop out of school. When he changed his mind.
> (The second part is an adverbial clause or fragment.)
> *right*: Just as he was about to drop out of school, Vadim changed his mind.

> *wrong*: Gabrielle studied long hours to improve her grades. Which happened in a short time.
> (The second part is a dependent clause; it cannot stand alone.)
> *right*: By studying long hours, Gabrielle quickly improved her grades.

PUNCTUATION BETWEEN CLAUSES

207. Do not join independent clauses with a comma alone.

    wrong: Felix took the test three times, he failed the test.
    right: Felix took the test three times, but he failed it each time.
        (See also **196**: comma + coordinating conjunction *but*.)
    right: Although Felix took the test three times, he failed it each time.
        (See also **195**: subordinate conjunction *although* + comma.)
    right: Felix took the test three times. Each time he took it, he failed it.
        (A period separates the thoughts.)
    right: Felix has failed the test three times now; as a result, he has to take it again.
        (See also **194**: semicolon + transitional conjunctive adverb *as a result* + comma.)

208. Do not write two sentences with no punctuation between them.

    wrong: We hope to move soon we've lived here too long.
    right: We hope to move soon; we've lived here too long.
        (Use a semicolon when the two thoughts flow or follow one from another.)
    right: We hope to move soon. I hear that Eastwick is a nice place to live.
        (Use a period when the thoughts are not closely related.)
    right: Because we've lived here so long, we're going to move soon.
        (Use a subordinate conjunction + a comma when one thought can depend on another; see also **195**.)
    right: We hope to move soon, but we haven't started looking for a new home yet.
        (Use a comma + a coordinate conjunction when the thoughts are related and of equal worth.)

SHIFTS

209. There should be no shifts of subject, number, tense, voice, mood, or point of view within a sentence. (See also **68; 71; 86**.)

    wrong: When you have a good car, one should take care of it.
    right: When one has a good car, one should take care of it.

    wrong: Everyone should be proud of their heritage.
    right: Everyone should be proud of his or her heritage.
    right: People should be proud of their heritage.

    wrong: The roaring of the crowd could be heard as we entered the concert hall.
    right: We heard the roar of the crowd as we entered the concert hall.

wrong: Before any testimony is accepted as fact, the committee must investigate the background of the witness.

right: Before accepting any testimony as fact, the committee must investigate the background of the witness.

DOUBLE NEGATIVES

210. Remember that double use of negative words in a sentence produces a positive meaning. Avoid double negatives wherever possible. *I am not uncomfortable* means *"I am comfortable." I don't know nothing,* on the other hand, is poor English and would be better written *I don't know anything* or *I know nothing.*

211. Modifiers such as *hardly*, *scarcely*, and *barely* carry negative meanings. They should not, therefore, be used as modifiers when there are other negating words in a sentence. (See also **132**.)

wrong: Edwina didn't hardly eat her lunch.
right: Edwina hardly ate her lunch.
right: Edwina didn't eat her lunch.

DEPENDENT CLAUSES

212. Noun clauses may be used anywhere nouns are used—as subjects, objects, etc. Do not use an adverbial clause where the construction of a sentence calls for a noun clause.

wrong: I heard where the weatherman said it was going to rain.
right: I heard that the weatherman said it was going to rain.
right: I heard that it was going to rain.

213. Do not use an adverbial clause where a noun or noun phrase is called for.

wrong: Success in this business is when you sell more than the other salespeople.
right: Success in this business means selling more than the other salespeople.
right: Success in this business means more sales than the other salespeople make.

WORD ORDER

Many English sentences use various word order schemes in order to gain emphasis. While there is no fixed pattern that one must follow, the normal order for an unremarkable sentence is subject, predicate, indirect object, direct object, adverbial modifiers.

214. Do not use adverbial modifiers to separate predicates from their direct or indirect objects.

> *wrong*: We went last week to Detroit.
>   *right*: Last week we went to Detroit.
>   *right*: We went to Detroit last week.

> *wrong*: Throw Mama down the stairs her hat. (This may result in injury.)
>   *right*: Throw Mama's hat down the stairs.

215. The order of words in a sentence may be vital to the intended meaning.

> *wrong*: Throw me a kiss from the bus. (Is the bus throwing the kiss?)
>   *right*: Before the bus leaves, look out the window and throw me a kiss.

MISLEADING MISPLACEMENTS

216. Single words, when misplaced, may be misleading.

> Last week I almost lost $100. (No money was lost.)
> Last week I lost almost $100. (A lot of money was lost.)

217. Phrases, when misplaced, may be misleading.

> Penelope held the cat with a smile. (Who is smiling, Penelope or the cat?)
> With a smile on her face, Penelope held the cat. (Clearly Penelope is smiling.)

> Last night I went to see Governor Brown in a new skirt. (Who was wearing the new skirt?)
> Last night I put on my new skirt and then went to see Governor Brown. (Clearly the speaker is wearing the new skirt.)

218. Clauses, when misplaced, may be misleading.

> When she was seven years old, Kate's aunt got the measles. (Who was seven when she contracted the measles?)
> When Kate was seven years old, her aunt got the measles.

> She put the letter as I was leaving in my pocket. (Leaving in a pocket?)
> As I was leaving, she put the letter in my pocket.

219. Modifying elements, when misplaced, may be misleading.

> Difficulties confronted Mr. Watkins which must be solved. (Is it Mr. Watkins who must be solved?)
> Difficulties which must be solved confronted Mr. Watkins.

We ate the bread which Edna baked in less than a minute. (Did she bake the bread in less than a minute?)

It took us less than a minute to eat the bread which Edna had made.

DANGLING SENTENCE ELEMENTS

Some misplacements of modifiers and verbals are said to be *dangling*, meaning that they relate to no clear part of the sentence. It may be necessary to rewrite sentences in order to avoid problems with dangling elements.

220. Participles should always modify something. (See also 128.)

> Walking down the path, the flowers can be seen in all their glory. (Who's walking?)
> If one walks down the path, one can see the flowers in all their glory.

> Completely frozen, we removed the ice trays from the freezer. (Who or what was frozen?)
> When the ice was completely frozen, we removed the ice trays from the freezer.

221. Gerunds must be properly placed. Watch passive voice constructions, to see that any gerunds are in their proper places.

> Swimming, my back was hurt. (Was the back swimming?)
> My strenuous swimming brought about a back injury.

> Moving the bureau, my back was hurt. (*Moving* is out of place.)
> I hurt my back while I was moving the bureau.

222. Infinitives must refer to something.

> To get here, a short cut had to be taken. (The infinitive is dangling.)
> We had to take a short cut to get here.

> To appreciate life, friends are needed. (another needless dangle)
> We need friends in order to appreciate life.

LOGIC

223. Be sure to arrange the thoughts in a sentence in a logical order.

> *illogical*: We mixed the batter, applied the icing, and baked the cake. (Icing is the last step in cake baking.)
> *logical*: We mixed the batter, baked the cake, and then applied the icing.

224. Do not use an illogical sequence where something equals something else.

> *illogical*: Reading is a real problem among the illiterate. (Since the illiterate cannot read, reading cannot be a problem. It is the lack of ability to read that is the problem.)

SUBORDINATION

225. Do not place the main or principal thought of a sentence in a subordinate position. The purpose of subordinate conjunctions is to introduce dependent clauses.

> *poor*: The car slowly chugged to a halt as I realized we had run out of gas.
> (*As* should not be used to introduce a main idea.)
> *better*: As the car slowly chugged to a halt, I realized we had run out of gas.

226. Use the correct subordinate conjunction.

> *wrong*: The reason he is fat is because he doesn't exercise
> (A reason cannot be *because*.)
> *right*: The reason he is fat is that he doesn't exercise.

227. Do not use subordinate conjunctions that may nullify the subordination.

> *wrong*: I want to buy a new suit but which is too expensive.
> (*But* has no place in this sentence. The two ideas are not of equal rank; one depends on the other. Thus, they cannot be connected by a coordinate conjunction.)
> *right*: I want to buy a suit which is too expensive.

228. Do not use a coordinate conjunction where a subordinate one is appropriate.

> *poor*: I am going to be late for work, and my car won't start.
> *better*: I am going to be late for work because my car won't start.

SENTENCE PATTERNS

229. Once a sentence pattern has been established, it should be continued.

> *Example*: *She dances well, she skates well, she runs well, and she skis well.*

Here the style of the writer is to repeat the subject + verb + adverb pattern in a list. Note the commas between the groupings and the *and* between the next-to-last and the last groupings.

230. An article or preposition that applies to all parts or members of a series must be used only before the first term, or it may be repeated before each.

> Sharon went to the post office, to the supermarket, to the drugstore, and to the library.
>
> Sharon went to the post office, the supermarket, the drugstore, and the library.
>
> Sharon went to the post office, supermarket, drugstore, and library.

PARALLELISM

231. A pair or a series of coordinate units should be of the same kind—nouns, adjectives, infinitives, etc.—not a mixture. The sameness of grammatical structure aids in the clarity, smoothness, and coherence of a sentence.

> *wrong*: It was cold, dark, and there was too much wind.
> (The list begins with two adjective complements, so it should continue with them.)
> *right*: It was cold, dark, and windy.

> *wrong*: Ice skating is more exciting than to roller-skate.
> (A gerund is being compared with an infinitive.)
> *right*: Ice skating is more exciting than roller skating.

> *wrong*: The motor sputtered, coughed, and then it was stopped.
> (There are two active voice verbs in a row, then a passive voice one.)
> *right*: The motor sputtered, coughed, and stopped.

232. It may be necessary to repeat a word to ensure parallelism. (See also **175; 177**.)

> *unclear*: We called our father and boss.
> *clear*: We called our father, and then we called our boss.
> *clear*: We called the man who is our father and boss.

> *unclear*: She wrote to her sister and roommate
> *clear*: She wrote to her sister and to her roommate.

233. Correlative conjunctions (*either . . . or, not only . . . but also*, etc.) should be used only in sentences with parallel structures. (See also **199**.)

> *wrong*: Roberta is not only a good secretary, but also she is able to organize things well.
> (The coordinate conjunction *but* should connect two predicate nominatives.)
> *right*: Roberta is not only a good secretary, but also a fine organizer.

SUBJECT-PREDICATE AGREEMENT

234. The subject of a sentence must agree with its predicate in number. Singular subjects take singular verbs; plural subjects take plural verbs. Present tense singular verbs in the third person end in *s*.

    The dog barks.   The dogs bark.

235. When words, phrases, or parenthetical expressions appear between the subject and predicate, ignore them for the purpose of agreement.

    Tammy, as well as her two cousins, calls me every day.
    (Tammy . . . calls me every day.)

    My two aunts, along with their cat Peter, visit me every Sunday.
    (My two aunts . . . visit me every Sunday.)

    Each of the plans has merit.
    (Each . . . has merit.)

    The performance of the three dancers was excellent.
    (The performance . . . was excellent.)

236. Verbs agree with their subjects even when the normal word order is reversed.

    Does either of the two applicants seem qualified?
    Have the workers voted on their new union pact?

237. *Here* and *there*, used as expletives, are introduction words; they are never subjects of sentences. (See also **202**.) Look elsewhere in sentences that use these words in order to find the true subjects.

    There is a crow on that tree limb. (subject: *crow*)
    There are 103 known chemical elements. (subject: *elements*)
    Here is my book.
    Here are my books.

238. When the subject and the predicate nominative are different in number, be sure that the verb agrees with the subject.

    Jelly beans are his favorite candy.
    Books are Janet's true passion.
    The present I liked best was the candlesticks.

239. When the subject is a unit of measurement, an amount, or the start of a mathematical equation, the predicate is singular when it is thought of as a whole, but plural when it is considered as a number of separate units. (See also **2**.)

    Three days is enough to complete the project. (singular)
    Two miles is the distance we need to walk. (singular)

Fifty dollars is not enough. (singular)
Three days are holidays this month—the 11th, the 16th, and the 27th. (plural)
These last three weeks have been full of surprises. (plural)
There are fifty ones (50 one-dollar bills) in this envelope. (plural)
Twelve feet is the length of this carpet. (singular)
One hundred ninety pounds is what I weighed when I started my diet. (singular)

240. When a fraction or percentage is used as a subject, the term following the *of* determines whether the predicate is singular or plural.

Two-fifths of our profits go to reinvestment. (*profits* is plural)
Three-fourths of the house is now ready. (*house* is singular)
Fifty percent of his crop is soy beans. (*crop* is singular)
Twenty-five percent of the students work after school. (*students* is plural)

241. A collective noun (a word that refers to a group or collection of things or people) takes a singular predicate when it is thought of as a unit and a plural predicate when the individual elements in the group are being considered. (See also **1a; 1b**.)

The jury has been out for 12 hours. (one unit—singular)
The jury are discussing the case among themselves. (separately considered—plural)

The crowd was large and disorderly.
The crowd were fighting among themselves.

242. Titles of books, articles, plays, etc., and names of companies, countries, and organizations take singular predicates even if their titles appear to be plural.

The Immigrants is a fine Bergman film.
The Netherlands is located in western Europe.
Passages, by Gail Sheehy, was on the best-seller list for months.
Merrill, Lynch, Pierce, Fenner, and Smith is a large brokerage house.
The Girls Scouts has its headquarters near my office.

243. When *number* is used as a subject and is followed by an *of* phrase, it is singular when preceded by *the* and plural when preceded by any other word. (See also **2c**.)

The number of incidents of robbery has risen.
A number of criminals have been caught.

244. Ideas that are collective in nature but plural in form take singular subjects.

> Ham and cheese on rye bread is my favorite sandwich.
> Bacon and eggs is what he always orders at that café.

245. Some noun subjects are always singular and require singular verbs; some noun subjects are always plural and require plural verbs. (See also 3; 4.)

> Economics is that professor's specialty. (singular)
> Politics plays a large part in their daily lives. (singular)
> The deceased's remains were divided among his children. (plural)
> The tactics she employed were highly effective. (plural)

246. When two or more subjects are joined by *and*, the predicate is plural.

> Eileen and Marge come to class together.
> Her ability and general understanding serve her well.

247. When two subjects are joined by *or* or *nor*, the predicate agrees with the nearer subject.

> My aunt or my uncle is likely to be there. (. . . uncle is . . .)
> Either the workers or the manager is wrong. (. . . manager is . . .)
> Neither the coach nor the players were happy with the schedule.
> (. . . players were . . .)
> Either Ginger or her daughters are going to repair the garage door.
> (. . . daughters are . . .)
> Neither the children nor their mother has flown before. (. . . mother has . . .)

248. A relative pronoun is singular or plural depending on its antecedent. (See also 32.)

> The people elect their representatives who speak for them in Congress. (representatives/who speak)
> He is one of the gardeners who work in our school's yard. (gardeners/who work)
> She is the only one, out of the entire group, who understands the problem. (one/who understands)
> Lucy is the potter who works in that craft shop. (potter/who works)

249. Some indefinite pronouns are always singular and require singular verbs; some are always plural and require plural verbs. (See also 35; 37.)

> It isn't twins, is it?
> Much of what you say makes sense to me.
> Has anybody seen my hat?
> Several have applied for the job.
> Both of your reasons are sound.

250. The indefinite pronouns *all*, *any*, *more*, *most*, *none*, and *some* may be singular or plural depending on their use.

> Most of the money was recovered. (noncountable—singular)
> Most of the gems were recovered. (countable—plural)
> Is all of the cotton picked? (noncountable—singular)
> Are all of the bales of cotton ready to be shipped? (countable—plural)

251. *Every* and *many a*, when used before a subject, require singular verbs.

> Every student, teacher, and staff member was asked to contribute.
> Many a college student wishes he'd studied harder in school.

PRONOUN-ANTECEDENT AGREEMENT

A pronoun must agree with its antecedent in number and gender. The section on subject-predicate agreement (234–251) will be useful to you in this important area; review it carefully. Thoroughly review the sections on pronouns and case and on pronouns and their antecedents (41–53;120).

252. Pronoun-antecedent reference must be clear, not vague or ambiguous.

> *unclear*: He talked to Dennis and Tom last night and he said that he got the job. (Who said that who got the job?)
> *clear*: When he talked to Dennis and Tom last night, he told them that he got the job.

> *unclear*: I hear that in England they drink a lot of tea.
> *clear*: I hear that the English drink a lot of tea.

> *unclear*: She put the pencil sharpener on the table that her brother had bought. (Did he buy the table or the pencil sharpener?)
> *clear*: She put the pencil sharpener that her brother had bought on the table.

> *unclear*: Fritz was in bad shape, which we could see from his facial expression.
> *clear*: Fritz was in bad shape. We could see the pain through his facial expression.

DIRECT AND INDIRECT DISCOURSE

Direct discourse is the direct quoting of a speaker or writer; quotation marks are used to set off the quoted words.
Indirect discourse is the indirect quoting of a speaker or writer, using such introductory words as *say*, *tell*, *think*, etc. No quotation marks are used. The verbs *answer*, *declare*, *observe*, *remark*, etc., are also used to report indirectly on someone's thoughts or words.

253. There is an exact sequence of tenses that must be followed in English sentences. In complex sentences, the verb in the subordinate clause must agree with the verb in the main clause. Note the tense changes that must be made in indirect discourse to ensure this agreement.

a. The present and future change to the past.

> *direct*: Rheba said, "I meet her here every day at three o'clock."
> *indirect*: Rheba said she met her there every day at three o'clock.

> *direct*: Lolita asked, "Will you meet me next Wednesday?"
> *indirect*: Lolita asked if I would meet her next Wednesday.

b. The present progressive changes to the past progressive.

> *direct*: She said, "I can't talk; I'm eating dinner now."
> *indirect*: She said she couldn't talk; she was eating dinner then.

c. The past changes to the past perfect.

> *direct*: Art said, "Paul really knew me well, Geraldo."
> *indirect*: Art told Geraldo that Paul had really known him well.

d. The past progressive changes to the past perfect progressive.

> *direct*: Ed said, "I was just waiting for a chance to talk to you."
> *indirect*: Ed declared that he had just been waiting for a chance to talk to us.

254. In the above examples, note the need for other types of changes in the use of pronouns and time words when changing from direct to indirect discourse. In the first example in 253*a*, *I* and *here* change to *she* and *there*. In 253*b*, *I* and *now* change to *she* and *then*. In 253*c*, *me* changes to *him*; the indirect object, *Geraldo*, changes position, becoming the indirect object of the main verb. In 253*d*, *I* and *you* change to *he* and *us*.

255. The past forms of auxiliaries are used to agree with the past forms of main clause verbs. (See also 92.)

> He said, "I can drive." He said he could drive.
> She said, "I must leave." She said she had to leave.

256. *a*. Commands in indirect discourse are expressed by the infinitive.

> *direct*: Martin cried out: "Stop that!"
> *indirect*: Martin told them to stop it.

> *direct*: Reggie exclaimed, "Don't push me again!"
> *indirect*: Reggie forcefully told them not to push him again.

b. Questions in indirect discourse are expressed as statements.

> *direct*: Alice asked, "Where does the producer live?"
> *indirect*: Alice asked where the producer lived.

      direct: "What time is it?" June inquired.
indirect: June wanted to know what time it was.

c. Questions with no question words may require the introduction of *if* or *whether* in indirect discourse.

      direct: Nuri asked, "Is my brother here?"
indirect: Nuri asked if her brother were there.

      direct: "Will she still be working after her baby is born?" Yasar asked.
indirect: Yasar asked whether she would still be working after her baby was born.

EXERCISES
(Answers are on pages 167–168.)

A. Circle the word or words in parentheses that make the sentence correct.

1. We raced to the depot and barely (*made, didn't make*) it to the train on time.

2. She told me (*where, that*) she was working at the Tom Thumb Deli.

3. Mrs. Curry opened (*this morning the mail, the mail this morning*) with her new letter opener.

4. I admitted that the reason I was taking math this summer was (*because, that*) I had failed it last semester.

5. Your greeting card arrived late, (*because, and*) the post office was on strike all last week.

6. New England is lovely in the winter, in the spring, (*the, in the*) summer, and in the fall.

7. The editor was bold, sassy, and (*aggressive, had an aggressive manner*).

8. (*Has, Have*) either of you done this before?

9. The view that I enjoyed most (*was, were*) the redwood trees in the northern forests.

10. Eighty percent of the seats on this train (*is, are*) occupied.

11. The United States (*comprises, comprise*) 6 percent of the world's population.

12. Here (*is, are*) your ticket and a magazine to take on your trip.

13. This is one of the questions that (*is, are*) going to be on the test.

14. Each of the twins (*has, have*) decided to grow a beard.

15. Some of the pollution (*has, have*) been caused by burning trash.

16. Many a person in your position (*wishes, wish*) she'd done things differently.

17. Michael said that he (*saw, had seen*) Al Pacino in a restaurant last week.

18. Yuan said he (*can't, couldn't*) get an earlier flight than the one tomorrow morning.

19. She stopped, then asked what day it (*is, was*).

20. Wendy wanted to know (*if her package had arrived, had her package arrived*).

B. Underline the word, phrase, or clause that is misplaced or misused in each of the following sentences. Then, in the space provided, write the sentence using proper word order and proper form.

1. He washed the crystal goblets his mother had given him gently. _____

_____

2. We had been talking to the lady on the bus with twins when you got on. _____

_____

3. We discovered an old antique shop wandering around the old part of town. _____

_____

4. When he was 20, Norman's father gave him a rifle. _____

_____

5. Eldridge noticed a misleading clause in the agreement that was right near the end. _____

_____

6. Strolling through the Tivoli Gardens, there are many lovers holding hands. _____

_____

7. Using the book of synonyms, he found the right word. ____

_____

8. The Koskoffs mailed their letters, walked to the post office, and bought some stamps. _____

_____

9. You might as well look at these prints now, and you are already here. _____

_____

10. He was a bully, an egotist, and foolish. _____

_____

11. Danny Ainge is not only a good baseball player, but he's also good at basketball. _____

_____

C. Write the correct form of the verb in parentheses in the space provided. (Be sure that the subject and predicate agree.)

Example: (go) On Tuesdays he usually ____*goes*____ to the hockey games.

1. (*seem*)   The sun _____ to rise in the east.

2. (*come*)   The people in our city _____ from many varied ethnic backgrounds.

3. (*be*)   _____ either of the skiers from Austria?

4. (*be*)   The femur, as well as all the tarsal bones,

    _____ in the leg.

5. (*be*)   There _____ several robberies in our neighborhood in the past few weeks.

6. (*be*)   Potatoes _____ the one food they serve with every meal.

7. (*be*)   Twelve divided by six _____ two.

8. (*be*)   Five pounds _____ what the scale says your watermelon weighs.

9. (*be*)   Twenty miles _____ marked off in half-mile segments along the path. They are visible even at night.

10. (*drink*)   Twenty-five percent of the beer drinkers

    _____ seventy-five percent of the beer.

11. (*suffer*)   The West Indies _____ from devastating hurricanes every year.

12. (*have*)   Woodward and Lothrop _____ a special sale on back-to-school clothes today.

13. (*rise*)   The number of accidents at that street cor-

    ner _____ dramatically on weekends.

14. (*be*)   Toast and coffee _____ her standard breakfast when she's on a diet.

15. (*be*)   Mathematics _____ my best subject this year.

16. (*fit*) _____ your trousers _____ well, or are they too tight?

17. (*keep*) The howling wind and the freezing cold often _____ us indoors for days at a time.

18. (*have*) Either the diode or the batteries _____ _____ worn out.

19. (*cater*) The Moldavis are the ones who always _____ our dinners.

20. (*go*) Something always _____ wrong when we try this recipe.

21. (*realize*) Few _____ the importance of the mission.

22. (*sit*) Some of the workers _____ idly, while others work hard.

23. (*feel*) Every member of our club _____ _____ indebted to Mr. Guardino for his support.

24. (*arrange*) The garden club usually _____ _____ tours of local gardens around this time of year.

D. Change each of the following sentences from the direct discourse form to the indirect discourse form.

> *Example*: She said, "I won't go."
> *She said she wouldn't go.*

1. "I went to your doctor for a second opinion on my problem,"

   Marilyn said. _____

   _____

2. Dick replied, "I'm sick because of those canned pears." ____

_____

_____

3. "I'm not going because no one else is going," explained Meredith. _____

_____

4. Martina said, "I won the first set, but then I folded." _____

_____

_____

5. "I was going to soccer practice," Jules said, "when I got hit by a car." _____

_____

_____

6. Owen shouted, "I'm here now!" _____

_____

7. Sean boasted, "I may have the best collection in town." ____

_____

_____

8. "Get these fish off my table!" hollered Glen. _____

_____

9. "Who's the fairest in the land?" Snow White asked the mirror. _____

_____

10. Judy asked the doctor, "Will my baby be all right?" _____

_____

ANSWER KEY

The numbers in parentheses refer to rules in this section that cover the relevant points.

A.
1. made (211)
2. that (212)
3. the mail this morning (215)
4. that (226)
5. because (228)
6. in the (230)
7. aggressive (231)
8. Has (236)
9. was (238)
10. are (240)
11. comprises (242)
12. are (237;246)
13. is (248)
14. has (235;249)
15. has (250)
16. wishes (251)
17. had seen (253*c*)
18. couldn't (255)
19. was (256*b*)
20. if her package had arrived (256*c*)

B.
1. *Underline*: gently
   Possible rewrite: He gently washed the crystal goblets his mother had given him. (214)

2. *Underline*: with twins
   Possible rewrite: When you got on the bus, we had been talking to the lady with twins. (217)

3. *Underline*: wandering around the old part of town
   Possible rewrite: Wandering around the old part of town, we discovered an old antique shop. (219)

4. *Underline*: he/Norman
   Possible rewrite: When Norman was 20, his father gave him a rifle. (218)

5. *Underline*: in the agreement
   Possible rewrite: Eldridge noticed a misleading clause that was right near the end of the agreement. (217)

6. *Underline*: Strolling through the Tivoli Gardens
   Possible rewrite: Many lovers can be seen strolling through the Tivoli Gardens holding hands. (220)

7. *Underline*: Using the book of synonyms
   Possible rewrite: He found the right word by using the book of synonyms. (221)

8. *Underline*: mailed their letters
   Possible rewrite: The Koskoffs walked to the post office, bought some stamps, and mailed their letters. (223)

9. *Underline*: and

   Possible rewrite: You might as well look at these prints now since you are already here. (228)

10. *Underline*: foolish

    Possible rewrite: He was a bully, an egotist, and a fool. (231)

11. *Underline*: he's also good at basketball

    Possible rewrite: Danny Ainge is not only a good baseball player, but also a good basketball player. (223)

C.
1. seems (234)
2. come (235)
3. Is (236)
4. is (235)
5. have been (237)
6. are (238)
7. is (239)
8. is (239)
9. are (239)
10. drink (240)
11. suffers (242)
12. has/is having (242)
13. rises (243)
14. is (244)
15. is/has been (245)
16. Do, fit (245)
17. keep (246)
18. have (247)
19. cater (248)
20. goes (249)
21. realize (249)
22. sit (250)
23. feels (251)
24. arranges (241)

D.
1. Marilyn said she had gone to my doctor for a second opinion on her problem. (253c)
2. Dick replied that he was sick because of those canned pears. (253a)
3. Meredith explained that she wasn't going because no one else was going. (253b)
4. Martina said that she had won the first set, but then she had folded. (253c)
5. Jules said that he had been going to soccer practice when he got hit by a car. (253d)
6. Owen shouted that he was there then. (254)
7. Sean boasted that he might have the best collection in town. (255)
8. Glen hollered at them to get those fish off his table. (256a)
9. Snow White asked the mirror who the fairest in the land was. (256b)
10. Judy asked the doctor if her baby would be all right. (256c)

Punctuation,
Capitalization,
and Abbreviations

Punctuation, Capitalization, and Abbreviations

APOSTROPHE

(See also **7; 10; 12–22; 42; 87; 91; 103; 168.**)

257. Use an apostrophe to indicate possession.

Jim's coat	the boss's desk
the woman's dress	the bosses' desks
the women's dresses	the babies' diapers
everyone's goal	somebody else's order

258. Use an apostrophe in a contraction to show that two words have been contracted into one.

I have	I've	will not	won't
she would	she'd	I am	I'm

259. Use an apostrophe for the plurals of letters, numbers, and symbols.

t's   14's   -'s   ½'s

260. Use apostrophes for quotations inside other quotations.

He said, "I'm not certain that I understood you when you asked, 'What are the dates of your trip?'"

261. To show joint ownership, use *'s* after the last name only. To show separate ownership, use *'s* after each name.

Donnie and Marie's records (joint ownership; they own them together)
Donnie's and Marie's records (separate ownership; each has records)

262. Note that an apostrophe is sometimes used to indicate the current century. A person born in 1933 might say: *I was born in '33.*

Do you remember the terrible snowstorm of '67?

COLON

263. Use a colon to introduce a list given after such words as *the following, as follows*, etc.

She asked for the following articles: an axe, a hammer, an awl, and a saw.
Our main considerations are as follows: safety, speed, and glamour.

Do not use a colon if a verb or preposition precedes the list.

The colors I chose were red, green, blue, and white.
This design comes in silk, satin, and cotton.

264. Use a colon in a business letter after the salutation.

> Dear Sirs:
> To whom it may concern:

265. Use a colon to introduce a long or formal quotation.

> In his speech to the United Nations, Mr. Teng said: "I come here
> today . . . ."

COMMA

(See also 136; 194; 195; 196; 200; 207; 208.)

266. Use a comma before a coordinate conjunction in a compound sentence.

> You do not have to pay anything extra, nor do you even have to be here
> in order to win.
> I came to work early, but no one was here.

267. Use a comma after an adverbial clause has introduced a sentence.

> As I started to answer the phone, the doorbell rang.
> After he bought the morning newspaper, he went to the station.

268. Use a comma after an introductory word or phrase.

> Since you asked, I will tell you.
> Unfortunately, we lost her address.
> By using a hot comb for 30 minutes, she straightened her hair.
> In accordance with your instructions, we are sending you the telegram.

269. Use commas to set off words or phrases that are not vital to the meaning
of the sentence.

> His allegation, which may not be true, brought him fame.

270. Use commas to set off or enclose words that have been loosely or paren-
thetically inserted into a sentence.

appositives:	Chris Photakis, my dentist, lives in Newark.
direct address:	Here, Mr. Reagan, is your certificate.
yes and no:	No, I've never been there. Yes, you have.
absolute phrases:	The game over, we all went home.
understood words:	Mary is the blonde; Carla, the brunette.
parenthetical expressions:	We wondered, however, how we were going to escape. The entire set, each piece handmade, took years to assemble.

271. Use commas with addresses, letters, degrees, and dates.

dates:	Tuesday, November 20, 1940
addresses:	318 First Street, Sacramento, California
degrees:	John Burke, Ph.D., has written this book.
friendly letters:	Dear Sweetie,
letter closings:	Sincerely,

272. Use a comma to prevent confusion or to ensure clarity.

Upstairs, the windows were creaking.
Jan, Michael, Vincent, and I will accompany you. (5 people)
Jan Michael Vincent and I will accompany you. (3 people)

273. Use commas to separate words, phrases, or clauses in a series.

We ordered a hamburger, French fries, apple pie, and a Coke.
He awoke, ate his breakfast, got dressed, and went to work.

274. Use a comma to separate a short, informal direct quotation from the rest of the sentence.

Nancy asked, "How many were in your class?"
"Please spend the night," Paul urged.
"Freedom," she sang, "is just another word for nothing left to lose."

275. Use commas to separate adjectives of equal rank that modify the same noun.

She wore a soft, brightly colored, warm, woolen sweater.
The method is fast, efficient, and inexpensive.

276. Use commas with tag ending questions. (See also **94**.)

Tokyo is north of here, isn't it?
You aren't finished school yet, are you?

DASH

277. Use dashes to show a break in thought within a sentence.

I'll meet you at six o'clock—no sooner, no later—to exchange the merchandise.

278. Use dashes to set off an appositive or a parenthetical expression to indicate more force than there would be with commas.

The senator—the one we've all been waiting to see—is waiting outside.
If you want to succeed—really succeed—you must study hard.

279. Use a dash to introduce a phrase that summarizes the preceding part of a sentence.

> Smoking, drinking, and lack of sleep—these are all causes of your nervousness.

EXCLAMATION POINT

(See also **203**.)

280. Use an exclamation point after an interjection, a statement of strong feeling, or an emphatic command.

> Darn! Hurray! Bill Green for mayor!
> Call now! Don't miss this exciting offer!

HYPHEN

(See also **10; 15**.)

281. Use a hyphen in compound numbers from twenty-one through ninety-nine.

> thirty-eight three hundred sixty-four

282. Use a hyphen in compound nouns and adjectives to show that they are functioning with the force of a single word. (See also **137**.)

> mother-in-law a well-known author
> self-centered up-to-the-minute news

283. Use a hyphen to divide syllables at the end of a line of writing or typing.

PARENTHESES

284. Use parentheses to set off a part of a sentence that is not vital to the meaning of the sentence and that has a thought that is independent of the sentence.

> Washington promised to sell Peking a communications satellite (to be launched by NASA from Cape Canaveral) by the end of the year.
> The office space they were looking at (about 900 square meters) was located in the best part of town.

PERIOD

(See also **207; 108**.)

285. Use a period after a complete thought, whether the thought is declarative, imperative, elliptical, or indirect.

> I came early.
> Let's go home.
> Have you seen him? Yes.
> He wanted to know if you had heard from Billy.

286. Use a period after abbreviations and initials, and to separate dollars and cents.

> Rev. Graham   9:15 A.M. $10.95

287. Use periods in a series to show omission (also called an ellipsis).

> She visits her parents in West Virginia on weekends.
> She visits . . . on weekends.

QUESTION MARK

288. Use a question mark at the end of a direct quotation in which a question is asked.

> She asked, "How many were in your class?"

289. Use a question mark to ask a series of questions in a sentence; that is, use one after each question, even if the sentence is not complete.

> How long have you been here? Ten minutes? Twenty? Thirty?

290. Use a question mark after a direct question that calls for an answer in words; use a period after a request that is stated in question form but that calls for action rather than words.

> Has my loan been approved? (A yes or no answer is anticipated.)
> Will you send me your brochure. (Action is anticipated.)
> Would you follow me, please. (Action is anticipated.)

QUOTATION MARKS

(See also **252**.)

291. Use quotation marks to enclose the exact words of a speaker or writer.

> Pat said, "Let me know what I can do to help."

292. Use quotation marks to enclose nicknames or slang expressions.

> "Ratso" Rizzo hated his nickname.
> This stuff is a lot of "baloney."

293. Use quotation marks to cite parts of a complete work, when the larger work is italicized. (See also **299.**)

> Her latest article, "My Visit to Cambodia," appears in the most recent issue of *Newsweek*.

294. The placement of other punctuation marks at the end of quotations varies.

a. Place question marks and exclamation points inside the closing quotation marks only if the quoted material is a question or exclamation.

> The true question is, "Will we be able to afford it?"
> He asked, "Do you have time to do this job?"
> She screamed, "Oh, how exciting!"

b. Place question marks and exclamation points outside the closing quotation marks only if the entire sentence is a question or exclamation.

> What did he mean when he said, "The future is now"?
> Stop saying "I can't do it"!

c. Always place periods and commas inside the closing quotation marks.

> They both said, "Let's find a name for the puppy."
> "He who treasures freedom," wrote Goethe, "must daily win it anew."
> A good definition for the word *egress* is "exit."

d. Always place colons and semicolons outside the closing quotation marks.

> Stop in to say "Hello"; then take a tour of the plant.
> My music appreciation teacher calls these composers "The Big Three": Bach, Brahms, and Beethoven.

SEMICOLON

Semicolons may be thought of as midway between commas (which indicate pauses) and periods (which indicate full stops).

295. Use a semicolon between the independent clauses of a compound sentence when a conjunction is not used.

> The summers were wet; the winters were dry.
> Don't lose that key; it opens the large suitcase with my new clothes.

---

296. Use a semicolon to avoid confusion with numbers or other items in a list.

> The rates quoted me were $29.95; $32.50; $35.00; and $37.50.
> For the history test, memorize the following dates: July 4, 1776; January 1, 1863; and December 7, 1941.

297. Use a semicolon if a sentence is long and complicated, even if a conjunction is used.

> The day was long, tiring, and nerve-wracking; but we all pulled through, helped each other, and came out of it intact.

298. Use a semicolon before and a comma after a transitional conjunctive adverb that has been used to join two independent clauses. (See also **194**.)

> I wanted to repot my house plants; however, I couldn't find the potting soil.

UNDERLINE

299. Underline (underscore) titles of separate publications such as books, magazines, pamphlets, and newspapers. In print, italics take the place of underlining.

> His articles appeared regularly in The Maine Times last year.
> Her book, How to Live on Nothing, was recommended by the editors of the Whole Earth Catalog.
> Calvin Trillin is a regular contributor to The New Yorker.

CAPITALIZATION

300. Capitalize the first word of every sentence, the first word of every line of poetry, the first word of a direct quotation, and the first word of both the salutation and the complimentary closing of a letter.

> Dear Sara,   Dear Sirs: Yours sincerely,

301. Capitals are also used in the following instances:

> *abbreviations*: (See list **302**.)
> *adjectives derived from proper names*: Asiatic, Swiss, Napoleonic
> *all proper names*: Alan, Christine, Joan of Arc, Mao Tse-tung

buildings, organizations, government bodies, historical events: the World Trade Fair Center, the UN (United Nations), Congress, the Boston Tea Party, the World Cup

cities, countries, geographic areas, continents: Singapore, Kenya, Central America, Africa, the Sahel

common nouns when they are part of a specific proper name: Hill Street, Lake Tahoe, the Indian Ocean

days, months, holidays: Tuesday, February, Christmas

literary works and publications: the Koran, *The Tragedy of Hamlet*, "Ode on a Grecian Urn," the Declaration of Independence

names of religions, ethnic or racial groups, political parties, and languages: Buddhism, Hispanics, Democrats, Arabic

regions of a country (but not general directions): the South, the Northwest; We drove south, then we turned east.

specific courses of study (but not subjects unless they come from proper names): Psychology 101, accounting, Spanish, early American history

titles (particularly when they are followed by someone's name): Ms., Mr., Senator Hayakawa, Aunt Jean

ABBREVIATION

302. Study and learn the following abbreviations.

Years and Times of Day

Abbreviation	*Words*	*Meaning and Use*
A.D.	*anno domini*	Latin, after the birth of Christ; Columbus discovered America in A.D. 1492.
A.M.	*ante meridiem*	Latin, before noon; I awoke at 6:15 A.M.
B.C.	before Christ	the years before the birth of Christ, counting in reverse order; Aristotle was born in the year 384 B.C.
EST CST MST PST	Eastern Standard Time Central Standard Time Mountain Standard Time Pacific Standard Time	the principal time zones in the United States
P.M.	*post meridiem*	Latin, after noon; We eat dinner every day at 6:30 P.M.

Days of the Week

Mon.	Monday	**Fri.**	Friday
Tues.	Tuesday	**Sat.**	Saturday
Wed.	Wednesday	**Sun.**	Sunday
Thurs.	Thursday		

Months of the Year

Jan.	January	**Jul.**	July
Feb.	February	**Aug.**	August
Mar.	March	**Sept.**	September
Apr.	April	**Oct.**	October
May	May	**Nov.**	November
Jun.	June	**Dec.**	December

Jobs and Titles

appt. appointment
B.A. Bachelor of Arts (basic college degree)
CPA certified public accountant
DDS doctor of dental surgery (dentist)
expd. experienced
Jr. Junior
K thousand ("CPA needed to 26K" in a classified ad means that the salary for a CPA could go as high as $26,000 per year.)
M.A. Master of Arts (advanced college degree)
M.D. medical doctor
Mr. Mister
Mrs. Missus (variation of *mistress*, a title formerly used for married women)
Ms. title used for a female of any age
Ph.D. Doctor of Philosophy (advanced college degree)
RN registered nurse
Sr. senior

Real Estate

a/c air conditioned
apt. apartment
CAC central air conditioning
conv. convenient ("conv. schools and bus")

fl.	floor
fr.	from
incl. util.	including utilities (The rent quoted includes charges for water, gas, and electricity.)
kit.	kitchen
res. mgr./supt.	resident manager/superintendent
rms.	rooms
stu.	studio
wbf	wood-burning fireplace
w/w	wall-to-wall carpeting

Locations

Ave.	Avenue
bldg.	building
Blvd.	Boulevard
Dr.	Drive
Pkwy.	Parkway
Pl.	Place
P.O.	post office
Rd.	Road
RFD	rural free delivery (used in rural addresses)
Rte.	Route
Sq.	Square
St.	Street

Miscellaneous

AE	American Express
AM/FM	amplitude modulation/frequency modulation (radio bands)
Btu	British thermal units (used to measure cooling/heating potential
Co.	Company
C.O.D.	collect on delivery (to be paid for when delivered)
D&B	Dunn & Bradstreet (Wall Street firm that rates companies)
D.C.	District of Columbia (Washington)
e.g.	*exempli gratia* (for example)
encl.	enclosed
ESP	extrasensory perception
et al.	*et alii* (and others)
etc.	*et cetera* (and so on)
i.e.	*id est* (that is)
Inc.	Incorporated
IQ	intelligence quotient
Ltd.	Limited
MC	Master Card (credit card)

mph	miles per hour
ms	manuscript
P.S.	postscript
rpm	revolutions per minute (Records are available at 33, 45, or 78 rpms.)
S.S.	social security (identification number)
UHF	ultrahigh frequency (TV band)
UN	United Nations
U.S.	United States
V	Visa (credit card)
VHF	very high frequency (TV band)
vs.	*versus* (against; "In today's game it's New York vs. Boston.")

Symbols

/	for ("3/$1" means three items for one dollar.)
$	dollars
¢	cents
%	percent
#	number
@	for each
c/o	in care of
&	and

EXERCISES
(Answers are on pages 185–186.)

A. Circle the term in parentheses that makes the sentence correct.

1. My (*wifes'/wife's*) car keys fell behind the desk.

2. You don't need all those (+*s*/+*'s*) in your calculations.

3. That style of appliance was offered only (*in/in:*) white, avocado, and harvest gold.

4. Appropriately (*enough/enough,*) the chairman introduced the board members.

5. Her designer jeans (, *meticulously tailored,/meticulously tailored*) were noticed by everyone.

6. They vacationed in San Juan (, *Puerto Rico,/Puerto Rico*) this year.

7. The travel agent urged that we go to Argentina, Brazil, Paraguay (, *and/and*) Uruguay, in that order.

8. It is unlikely (*highly unlikely/—highly unlikely—*) that we'll see results from those tests in less than ten days.

9. Hurry, or you'll miss the grand (*finale./finale!*)

10. The booklet contained 14 (*easy to follow/easy-to-follow*) instructions.

11. Which of these two colors is more (*provocative!/provocative?*)

12. Did Deanna really say, "I don't want to live (*here?"/here"?*)

13. (*"Commas,"/"Commas"*) she said, "are useful writing tools."

14. You may have my seat if you (*wish,/wish;*) I'm moving to another part of the auditorium.

15. Those errors were costly to us (; *however,/however*) if you hadn't found the problem when you did, it would have cost a lot more.

16. Have you ever read the journal called (<u>Scientific American</u>/ "Scientific American")?

17. The author wrote, "(*This/this*) book is dedicated to my husband."

18. The group sang a lot of old, (*irish/Irish*) songs.

19. We should have your foundation laid by (*Labor Day/labor day*), Mr. Hall.

20. Look over there! I believe that's (*ambassador/Ambassador*) Dane.

B. Some of the following sentences require additional punctuation. If a sentence is already punctuated correctly, write *C* (correct) in the space provided. If a sentence requires additional punctuation, write *I* (incorrect) in the space provided and insert the correct marks.

Example: Last month's total was 8719 this
month's will be even higher.   __I__

Correction: Last month's total was 8719; this
month's will be even higher.

---

1. Heather didnt call until 10:15; we were very upset. _____

2. Both Cheryls and Tanya's horses are stabled at Mr. Lynch's ranch. _____

3. She requested the following presents for her birthday: a doll, a red wagon, and a tennis racket. _____

4. After the cross-country race, all she could say was, "I'm bushed." _____

5. The telethon now in its last two hours has already surpassed its fund-raising goals. _____

6. While we were eating the baby started to cry. _____

7. The 15-year-olds in our school are wearing bright, colorful, and expensive lipstick. _____

8. The thief was running toward you wasn't he? _____

9. Good looks, money, and talent—that movie star has everything. _____

10. Four hundred thirty five representatives serve in the lower house of Congress. _____

11. Harold Carmichael (6′9″, 285 lbs.) has been a star for the Eagles for many years. _____

12. We usually finish work at 4:45 PM. _____

13. She turned to Janet and said, "Do you come here often." _____

14. With his heavy accent, he sounded as if he were saying Hoppy bird day. _____

15. They opened branches in Caracas, Venezuela; Bogotá, Colombia; Quito, Ecuador; and La Paz, Bolivia. _____

C. Rewrite the following sentences, inserting whatever punctuation marks or capitalization is necessary to make them correct.

1. the rug has a place near its middle about two square feet where the nap is worn through. _____

   _____

2. lucia did you apply for that job in racine wisconsin. _____

   _____

3. the other day scotty said to me shes a 120 word per minute stenographer. _____

   _____

4. no mrs blume replied im not interested _____

   _____

5. the president was inaugurated on jan 20 he started working the same day _____

   _____

6. they told us to meet them at their offices on 16th st in washington d c _____

   _____

7. action speed and excitement this movie has everything ____

   _____

8. he asked dr keegle for the following supplies bandages tape some whole blood and four units of iv solution. _____

   _____

   _____

9. the lawyer an articulate broad shouldered woman addressed

   helens girl scout troop _____

   _____

10. my grandfather used to reminisce lord it hasnt been this cold

    since the winter of 38 _____

    _____

D. For each of the words on the left, find its definition on the right. Then write the letter in the blank.

a.	mph	1. _____	number
b.	CAC	2. _____	registered nurse
c.	Dr.	3. _____	Friday
d.	e.g.	4. _____	Junior
e.	Nov.	5. _____	Incorporated
f.	P.M.	6. _____	miles per hour
g.	PST	7. _____	after noon
h.	Jr.	8. _____	Drive
i.	kit.	9. _____	in care of
j.	#	10. _____	central air conditioning
k.	vs.	11. _____	November
l.	Fri.	12. _____	social security
m.	S.S.	13. _____	for example
n.	Inc.	14. _____	kitchen
o.	RN	15. _____	Pacific Standard Time
p.	c/o	16. _____	against

ANSWER KEY

The number in parentheses refers to the rule that covers this point.

A.
1. wife's **(257)**
2. +'s **(259)**
3. in **(263)**
4. enough, **(268)**
5. , meticulously tailored, **(269; 270)**
6. , Puerto Rico, **(271)**
7. , and **(273)**
8. —highly unlikely— **(277; 278)**
9. finale! **(280)**
10. easy-to-follow **(282)**

11. provocative? **(290)**
12. here"? **(294b)**
13. "Commas," **(294c)**
14. wish; **(295)**
15. ; however, **(298)**
16. <u>Scientific American</u> **(299)**
17. This **(300)**
18. Irish **(301)**
19. Labor Day **(301)**
20. Ambassador **(301)**

B.
1. I didn't **(258)**
2. I Cheryl's **(261)**
3. C **(263)**
4. C **(258; 267; 274)**
5. I telethon, hours, **(269)**
6. I eating, **(272)**
7. C **(275)**
8. I you, **(276)**

9. C **(279)**
10. I thirty-five **(281)**
11. C **(284)**
12. I P.M. **(286)**
13. I often?" **(288)**
14. I "Hoppy bird day." **(292)**
15. C **(296)**

C. Rules 295–301 apply to this exercise.

1. The rug has a place near its middle (about two square feet) where the nap is worn through.
2. Lucia, did you apply for that job in Racine, Wisconsin?
3. The other day Scotty said to me, "She's a 120-word-per-minute stenographer."
4. "No," Mrs. Blume replied, "I'm not interested."
5. The President was inaugurated on Jan. 20; he started working the same day.
6. They told us to meet them at their offices on 16th St. in Washington, D.C.
7. Action, speed, and excitement—this movie has everything.
8. He asked Dr. Keegle for the following supplies: bandages, tape, some whole blood, and four units of IV solution.
9. The lawyer, an articulate, broad-shouldered woman, addressed Helen's Girl Scout troop.
10. My grandfather used to reminisce, "Lord, it hasn't been this cold since the winter of '38!"

D. Rules for abbreviations are covered in **302**.

1. *j*	3. *l*	5. *n*	7. *f*	9. *p*	11. *e*	13. *d*	15. *g*
2. *o*	4. *h*	6. *a*	8. *c*	10. *b*	12. *m*	14. *i*	16. *k*

Review of
English Usage

Usage

Many words are confusing because of their closeness or similarity. Even native speakers have problems with many of these terms. Some cause problems because they are homonyms; that is, they sound alike when spoken, but they have different meanings. Others cause problems because their meanings are so similar that we must make distinctions in usage. Finally, there are terms that have identical meanings; they differ only in their idiomatic uses. You will note that many of these sets of terms appear in other sections of this text, too. They are repeated here for easy reference.

1. **ability**: the power to do something
   capacity: the power to hold or contain something
   > She has the *ability* to become a great poet.
   > This room's *capacity* is 350 people.
   > His *capacity* to eat lasagna seems endless.

2. **accede**: comply with
   exceed: surpass
   > I hope the judge *accedes* to our request for a speedy trial.
   > This year's sales *exceeded* last year's.

3. **accept** (*verb*): receive
   except (*preposition*): excluding, but, other than
          (*verb*): leave out
   > Did you *accept* their terms? Yes, *except* for the delivery date.
   > He was *excepted* from military service because of his poor eyesight.

4. **access**: admission
   assess: evaluate
   excess: a surplus, more than enough
   > You can gain *access* to the office by going through this door.
   > Their home was *assessed* at over $100,000.
   > We have an *excess* of rabbits; we'll have to sell a few.

5. **adapt** (*verb*): adjust or make suitable
   adept (*adjective*): skillful, proficient
   adopt (*verb*): choose and take as one's own
   > She had to *adapt* to the customs in her new homeland.
   > A good secretary is *adept* at handling business calls.
   > You'll save time if you *adopt* this new procedure.

6. **addition**: the joining of one to another
   edition: the whole number of copies printed at one time
   > Joe has the contract to build the new *addition* to City Hall.
   > Which *edition* of *Time* are you reading?

7. **advice** (*noun*): a recommendation or suggestion
   advise (*verb*): give counsel, recommend
   > My *advice* to you is to get a new job.
   > I *advise* you to find a new job.

8. **affect** (*verb*): influence or change
        (*noun*): emotional state of response
   effect (*verb*): bring about
        (*noun*): result
   > How does the weather *affect* you?
   > It surprised everyone to see that her *affect* was flat even though her
   >   mother had just died.
   > We're trying to *effect* a reconciliation between the two sides.
   > This will have a profound *effect* on me.

9. **after** (*preposition*): an introduction to time phrases
   afterward (*adverb*): later
   > I went to the post office *after* lunch.
   > I ate lunch, and *afterward* I went to the post office.

10. **agree to**: used with a thing
    agree with: used with a person, weather, or food
    > I *agree to* your conditions.
    > I *agree with* you. I don't *agree with* Jane.
    > This balmy Caribbean weather *agrees with* me.
    > That chili I ate doesn't *agree with* me; I feel ill.

11. **all**: whole, entire; used to indicate completeness
    each: used to indicate the separate members of a group
    every: used to indicate the unity of a group
    not all: part
    > *All* of the children are here. *All* the work is done.
    > *Each* member voted in accord with his or her conscience.
    > *Every* member participated in the debate.
    > *Not all* the members voted for acquittal. (Only some of them did.)

12. **all ready**: all were prepared
    already: previously, by this time
    > The papers are *all ready* to be signed.
    > I've *already* seen that film three times.

13. **already**: by this time, previously
    yet: so far
    > I've *already* finished my homework, have you? No, not *yet*.
    > Have you seen that film *yet*? Yes, I've *already* seen it twice.

14. **All right** is the correct form of this expression; it is the opposite of *all
         wrong*. Never use *alright*.

15. **all together**: all in one group or place
    altogether: entirely, completely
    > The papers are *all together* in a pile on the desk.
    > This dress is *altogether* too small for me.

16. **allusion**: a reference or indirect mention
    illusion: a deceptive or unreal image
    delusion: a false belief
    > Her *allusion* to his obesity offended him.
    > Were you fooled by the magician's *illusions*?
    > The patient's *delusion* was that he was invisible.

17. **almost**: very nearly, not quite
    most: the greater or greatest number
    > *Almost* everyone in our class owns an encyclopedia.
    > You'll find that definition in *most* dictionaries.

18. **also; too**: used in affirmative sentences
    either: used in negative sentences
    > I have a cat. I *also* have a dog.
    > Do you want a canary, *too*? No, and I don't want a gerbil *either*.

19. **alumna** (plural, *alumnae*): a female graduate
    alumnus (plural, *alumni*): a male graduate
    > She was an *alumna* of an all-girls college.
    > He was an *alumnus* of Harvard.

20. **all ways**: all methods
    always: at all times
    > We tried *all ways* of losing weight.
    > They *always* try to do their best.

21. **among**: used to compare three or more items
    between: used to compare two items
    > Let's keep this secret *among* the four of us.
    > Nothing can come *between* her and her husband.

22. **amoral**: not concerned with moral standards
    immoral: evil, contrary to moral standards
    unmoral: unable to distinguish moral standards
    > Animals are *amoral*; murderers are immoral; infants are *unmoral*.

23. **amount**: used with noncountable nouns
    number: used with countable nouns
    > We spread a large *amount* of manure on our garden.
    > A large *number* of members came late.

24. **anymore**: refers to something in the past, no longer happening
    still: refers to continuous action up to the present
    > Are you *still* active in your club? No, I'm not active *anymore*; I quit,
    > but my sister *still* belongs.

25. **any one**: a specific person or thing (always followed by *of*)
    anyone: anybody (in general)
    You may have *any one of* these three books.
    Has *anyone* seen Roger today?

26. **any way**: any manner
    anyway: in any case, nevertheless
    I'm not dissatisfied with this product in *any way*.
    It's late, but I hope she comes *anyway*.

27. **apt**: based on a strong or habitual tendency
    liable: emphasizing a bad outcome
    likely: expressing probability
    He's so clumsy, he's *apt* to break the cup.
    I'm *liable* to catch Diane's cold.
    They're *likely* to agree with you on that issue.

28. **as far as**: used with distance expressions
    until: used with time expressions
    They rode only *as far as* Westchester; we rode farther than that.
    We waited *until* 11:30, but he never came.

29. **bad**: *adjective*
    badly: *adverb*
    I feel *bad* because I have a *bad* cold.
    He drives *badly*.

30. **band**: group or company
    banned: forbidden
    A *band* of musicians is playing in the park.
    The publication was *banned* in that country.

31. **bare**: naked, uncovered; to reveal
    bear: an animal; to suffer or carry
    Without paintings, the room looked *bare*.
    The prosecution *bared* the facts to the jury.
    Our zoo has two polar *bears*.
    Please *bear* with me, I'll only be a few more minutes.

32. **beat**: refers to teams or opponents
    win: refers to games
    New York *won* the World Series by *beating* Los Angeles.

33. **billion**: in America and France: 1,000,000,000
    in Britain and Germany: 1,000,000,000,000

34. **blew**: past tense of *blow*
    blue: a color
    The wind *blew* fiercely.
    The sky is *blue*.

35. **borrow** or **lend**: Usage depends on direction. We borrow *from* someone or something, but we lend *to* someone or something.
    loan: a synonym for *lend*
    I want to *borrow* your pencil.
    Lend me a dollar, please.
    Loan me a dollar, please.

36. **born**: been given birth to
    borne: carried
    She was *born* in Poland.
    He has *borne* his burdens well.

37. **brake**: a device for slowing down
    break: rupture, shatter
    Stop! Put on your *brakes*!
    When did you *break* your glasses?

38. **bring**: Usage depends on direction. We bring something *toward* the speaker.
    take: We take something *away* from the speaker.
    Please *take* this dessert over to your grandmother's, and when you return, *bring* her laundry with you, so we can do it for her.

39. **canvas** (*noun*): heavy, rough cloth
    canvass (*verb*): survey, solicit votes
    Those old paintings were done on *canvas*.
    Let's *canvass* the inner city for Senator Shackleton.

40. **capital** (*adjective*): main or most important
    (*noun*): chief city in a state, province, or country; a sum of money
    capitol (*noun*): a domed building where a legislature meets (when this word is spelled with an upper-case *C*, it refers only to the official building of the United States Congress in Washington, D.C.)
    Proper nouns should be spelled with a *capital* letter.
    The phrase *capital punishment* means the death penalty.
    Canberra is the *capital* of Australia.
    How much *capital* have you invested in the company?
    The *capitol* in Columbia, South Carolina, resembles the *Capitol* in our nation's *capital*.

41. **cents**: the plural of *cent*, pennies
    sense: intelligence; to feel
    scents: aromas, odors
    The candy costs thirty *cents* (30¢).
    He knows better than to go there; he has good *sense*.
    I *sense* that you are upset about something.
    The *scents* of the various perfumes she uses filled the air.

42. **childish**: refers to a child's negative or unattractive qualities
childlike: refers to a child's positive or most attractive qualities
Cecilia is whining and generally behaving *childishly*.
Phoebe won our hearts with her haunting, *childlike* manner.

43. **cite** (*verb*): quote, bring forth as proof or authority
sight (*noun*): a vision, scene, view
       (*verb*): see
site (*noun*): plot of ground, place, location
To prove his point, he *cited* examples from the textbook.
The sunset this evening was a magnificent *sight*.
Columbus *sighted* land after being at sea for three months.
The *site* of the new stadium was once a parking lot.

44. **clothes**: garments
cloths: pieces of cloth
Her new *clothes* are fashionable.
He uses these old *cloths* for dusting.

45. **coarse** (*adjective*): rough, unrefined
course (*noun*): path; school subject; part of a meal
The *coarse* material scratched my skin.
My *course* of action is clear.
Did you take Ms. Goldman's *course* on literature?
The main *course* was baked fish.

46. **compare**: examine for similarities or resemblances
contrast: examine for differences
People always *compare* me with my brother.
The poverty of the slums *contrasts* sharply with the wealth of the suburbs.

47. **complement**: complete or fill something up
compliment: praise, express admiration
Your new black shoes *complement* the rest of your outfit.
Ed *complimented* her on her outstanding work.

48. **Controller** and **comptroller** are both used to describe the chief financial officer of an organization. The words are interchangeable.

49. **contemptible**: deserving of contempt
contemptuous: showing or exhibiting contempt
He is a *contemptible* person; no one likes him.
She was a *contemptuous* person; she was disdainful toward everyone.

50. **continual**: regularly, periodically repeated
continuous: without break, uninterrupted
The man in the audience *continually* interrupted the speaker.
It snowed *continuously* for five hours.

51. **core**: the central part
   corps: an organized group
   Let's get to the *core* of this meeting; why are you here?
   She served with the Peace *Corps* in Bolivia.

52. **correspondence**: letters (a noncountable noun)
   correspondents: letter writers (countable)
   I've received a lot of *correspondence* from his lawyers.
   Two other *correspondents* wrote to ask for the same data.

53. **counsel** (*verb*): give advice
   (*noun*): attorney
   council (*noun*): an assembly, a group of people
   consul (*noun*): an official of a foreign government
   She *counseled* her client to plead innocent.
   Bailey served as *counsel* for the defense.
   Graham was elected to the city *council* for a second term.
   The Danish *consul* gave us visas to visit for one month.

54. **credible**: believable
   creditable: praiseworthy
   credulous: gullible
   She told a *credible* story; no one doubted her.
   She told it in a *creditable* way; in fact, we applauded her.
   She admitted that she had always been a *credulous* person, believing
   everything she heard.

55. **definite**: specific and concrete
   definitive: final and complete
   We've made *definite* plans; I don't want to change them.
   He thought his work was to be the *definitive* study on Plato, but
   others proved him wrong.

56. **desert** (*verb*): abandon
   (*noun*): a dry, sandy wilderness
   dessert (*noun*): a sweet, last course at a meal
   The doe refused to *desert* her fawn even in the face of danger.
   The Sahara *Desert* occupies over 3 million square miles.
   We had blueberry pie for *dessert* last night.

57. **device** (*noun*): a mechanical invention
   devise (*verb*): plan or contrive
   We *devised* a new method of using this old *device*.

58. **die**: lose life
   dye: color
   These flowers are *dying* from lack of sunlight.
   When I came in, Eva was *dyeing* the curtains green.

59. **Different from** is the correct phrase to use in comparisons. Never use
   different than.

---

60. **disinterested**: not biased, impartial, without self-interest
uninterested: bored, not concerned, lacking interest
The jury professed to be a *disinterested* assembly, there only to hear the evidence. Not one of them, however, was *uninterested* in the case.

61. **do; make**: Both verbs have the same meaning of "accomplish," "bring into being," "perform," "carry out." The differences are idiomatic. Note these uses:

do the dishes   make a mistake
do errands   make meals (make lunch, dinner)
do exercises   make the bed
do the job   make a phone call
do (all forms of) housework   make a deposit
      make someone feel good

62. **emigrate**: leave one's country for another (*noun, emigrant*)
immigrate: come into a country from another (*noun, immigrant*)
Aga *emigrated* from Turkey to the United States.
When he arrived, he was called a Turkish *immigrant*.

63. **envelop** (*verb*): cover, surround completely
envelope (*noun*): a paper container for a letter
The fog *enveloped* our car, blinding us; we could not see the road.
What size *envelope* shall I put this check into?

64. **every day** (*adverb*): each single day
everyday (*adjective*): daily, common
I take the bus to work *every day*.
When I fish I forget my *everyday* cares.

65. **every one**: each single one (always followed by *of*)
everyone: everybody
Every one of the students passed the course.
I think you'll enjoy Leo Buscaglia; *everyone* does.

66. **famous**: favorably well known
infamous: unfavorably well known, notorious
Clint Eastwood is a *famous* movie star.
The notorious Jesse James became *infamous* by robbing banks.

67. **farther, farthest**: refers to distance or remoteness in space
further, furthest: refers to distance in time, degree, extent, or quantity
Arizona is *farther* from here than I thought.
Do you need *further* assistance?
This relationship has gone *further* than anyone expected.

68. **fewer**: used with countable nouns
less: used with noncountable nouns
Herbert smokes *fewer* cigars and drinks *less* coffee than he did before his illness.

69. **flowed**: past tense and participle form of *flow*
    flown: participle form of *fly*
    The river *flowed* swiftly.
    The storks *have flown* to Egypt to mate.

70. **forceful**: vigorous, aggressive, effective
    forcible: accomplished by force
    What a *forceful* and dynamic speaker she is!
    The police saw that the thieves had *forcibly* entered the house.

71. **formally**: ceremoniously, referring to manner
    formerly: previously, referring to time
    The butler *formally* announced the guests as they arrived.
    She was *formerly* the cruise director; now she's the captain.

72. **former**: the first of two items mentioned
    latter: the second of two items mentioned
    Kurt and Shirley are from opposite ends of the country; the *former* is
        from Portland, Maine, the *latter* is from Portland, Oregon.

73. **forth** (*adverb*): outward, onward, forward
    fourth (*adjective*): the next ordinal number after third
    "Go *forth* from this place and never return," the king said.
    This is the *fourth* time we've come to Disney World. We love it.

74. **fortuitous**: accidental, by chance
    fortunate: lucky
    How *fortuitous* to run into you here in Athens!
    We were indeed *fortunate* to find such a trouble-free car.

75. **good** (*adjective*): having positive or desirable qualities
    well (*adverb*): how something is done
        (*adjective*): being in good health, healthy
    Have a *good* time.
    She swims *well*.
    How *well* is your patient, doctor?

76. **gorilla**: one of the great apes
    guerrilla: an irregular soldier
    Our zoo has six *gorillas*.
    The *guerrillas* fought the government's army in the mountains.

77. **hanged**: past tense of *hang*; used with a person
    hung: past tense of *hang*; used with a thing
    The murderer was *hanged* for his crime.
    We *hung* the plant from the ceiling.

78. **healthful**: conducive to good health
healthy: possessing good health
  This is a *healthful* climate—clean air and plenty of sun.
  She had a *healthy* attitude about life. Her body was *healthy*, too, from good exercise and a proper diet.

79. **holy** (*adjective*): sacred
wholly (*adverb*): entirely
  Lourdes is a *holy* shrine.
  Mecca is a *holy* city.
  That driver is *wholly* responsible for the accident.

80. **human**: characteristic of men and women
humane: tender, kind, compassionate
  The medical students are studying *human* physiology.
  The commandant of the camp made sure that the prisoners were treated *humanely*.

81. **illegible**: difficult to read or decipher
ineligible: not qualified because of training or law
  My doctor's handwriting is almost *illegible*.
  She was *ineligible* for the position because she was only 14.

82. **imply**: hint or suggest (a giving activity)
infer: read into or draw a conclusion (a receiving activity)
  The speaker *implied* to the audience that it was late in the day.
  The audience *inferred* from what the speaker said that it was late in the day.

83. **incite** (*verb*): stir up
insight (*noun*): understanding
  The newspaper article *incited* our anger.
  We gained some valuable *insight* into the problem.

84. **incredible**: extraordinary, unbelievable; used with things
incredulous: not believing, skeptical; used with people
  June told an *incredible* story to an *incredulous*-looking crowd.

85. **ingenious**: clever, inventive
ingenuous: candid, honest
  It was such an *ingenious* device that it even shut itself off.
  The waitress had an *ingenuous* manner that reminded us of our five-year-old daughter's.

86. **intelligent**: smart, wise
intelligible: able to be understood, understandable
  She proved she was *intelligent* by scoring well on the IQ test.
  His slurred language was not *intelligible* to us.

87. **its**: possessive adjective
    it's: contraction for *it is*
    > The school announced *its* schedule for the fall.
    > *It's* time to go home.

88. **last**: the final
    latest: the most recent
    > We must missed the *last* flight of the day.
    > What's the *latest* news?

89. **lay** (*transitive verb*): put, place (*lay, laid, laying, laid*)
    lie (*intransitive verb*): rest, recline, remain (*lie, lay, laying, lain*)
    > *Lay* the books on the table.   The chicken *laid* an egg.
    > *Lie* down if you're tired.   The rug *lies* on the floor.

90. **learn**: acquire skills or knowledge
    teach: give or impart skills or knowledge
    > Students *learn* from teachers.
    > Teachers *teach* students.

91. **least**: smallest
    lest: for fear that
    > This is the *least* comfortable chair in the house.
    > I ran, *lest* I miss the bus.

92. **lessen** (*verb*): grow smaller
    lesson (*noun*): anything learned or studied
    > Our fears *lessened* as we became accustomed to the dark.
    > What *lesson* do we have for homework?

93. **leave**: allow or permit to remain; go away
    let: allow or permit; rent
    > Will you *leave* your keys on the table as you *leave*, please.
    > Will they *let* us in? *Let* me know, will you?
    > Our neighbors are planning to *let* their house while they're on vacation.

94. **loose** (*adjective*): not tied or tight, free
    　　　　(*verb*): release
    lose (*verb*): suffer a loss, cease having
    > These ropes are *loose*; we should tighten them.
    > *Loose* my chain, the dog seemed to say.
    > I hope you didn't *lose* my phone number.

95. **majority**: more than half the total
    plurality: the highest number within a great number but less than 50 percent of it
    > In our state, Samuels received 7 out of every 10 votes. Seventy percent is a clear *majority*. In another state, Samuels ran against several opponents; he won, but he received only 40 percent of the vote. In that case, his victory was by *plurality*. (The other candidates received 25 percent, 20 percent, and 15 percent of the votes, respectively.)

96. **many**: used with countable nouns
much: used with noncountable nouns
a lot of: used interchangeably with *many* and *much*
   Do you drink *much* wine? Do you drink *a lot of* wine?
   How *much*? How *many* glasses a day?
   Not *many*. I drink only one or two glasses a day.
   I do drink *a lot of* sodas, though.

97. **material**: goods or products
materiel: military term for supplies or equipment
   How much *material* will I need to make my curtains?
   The Army *Materiel* Command has ordered a total inventory of our supplies.

98. **may be** (*verb*): refers to possibility
maybe (*adverb*): perhaps
   I *may be* able to go with you after all.
   Maybe we should reconsider our decision.

99. **moral**: ethical issue involving right and wrong
morale: mental state involving courage and confidence
   Aesop's fables always end with a *moral*.
   They kept *morale* on the ship high by stopping in interesting ports.

100. **morn**: morning
mourn: grieve, express sorrow
   The *morn* brings a new day, a new spirit.
   Mother *mourned* father's death for a long time.

101. **no body**: no group (always followed by *of*); no corpse
nobody: not one person
   No body of workers is better qualified than the people in our factory.
   No body was found in the grave when they dug it up.
   Nobody has access to the files without Mr. Korenkiewicz's approval.

102. **passed** (*verb*; *past tense of* pass): moved from one state or condition to another
past (*noun or adjective*): gone by
   Genuine Risk *passed* all the other horses and won the race.
   Santayana said, "Those who cannot remember the *past* are condemned to repeat it."
   This *past* month seemed to pass quickly.

103. **patience**: calm endurance (noncountable noun)
patients: people under medical care (countable noun)
   It takes *patience* to weave a tapestry.
   Dr. Brogan's *patients* had to find a new dentist when she retired.

104. **percent** (also *per cent*): used with a number; parts per 100
    percentage: used for quantities; proportion
       Inflation ran at 18 *percent* last year.
       A large *percentage* of their income was from investments.

105. **personal**: private
    personnel: employees
       She had *personal* reasons for leaving early today.
       Our *personnel* office is looking for typists. Are you interested?

106. **practicable**: workable, feasible, able to be practiced
    practical: useful, valuable
       This project is not *practicable*; it won't work.
       That's a *practical* idea—it's sound and well reasoned.

107. **precede**: go before
    proceed: advance
       A *precedes* B in the alphabet.
       You may *proceed* across the street; the light is green.

108. **principal** (*noun*): director of a school; a sum of money; person in charge
          (*adjective*): main or most important
    principle (*noun*): rule, law, basic truth
       The *principal* at our high school made sure that we learned the *principles* of good citizenship. Indeed, it was her *principal* theme during our last year.

109. **prophecy** (*noun*): prediction
    prophesy (*verb*): foretell
       Her *prophecies* were often accurate; for example, she said it would rain today, and it did.
       He tried to make a living as a prophet, by *prophesying* the future.

110. **quiet**: still, without noise
    quite: entirely, altogether, positively
       It's much *quieter* in the country than in the city.
       Are you *quite* sure about that? Yes, I'm certain.

111. **raise** (*transitive verb*): lift, elevate; bear and rear children
    rise (*intransitive verb*): stand; get out of bed; increase in value
       Raise the window.
       She *raised* 12 children by herself.
       I *rise* (also *arise*) at eight o'clock every morning.
       AT&T stock *rose* six points last week.

112. **real** (*adjective*): genuine, having existence
    really (*adverb*): extremely, genuinely, in reality
       These shoes are made of *real* leather.
       I'm *really* glad to meet you.

113. **remember:** think of something with no assistance (only one person is involved in the action of this verb)
    remind: cause someone to think of something
    I *remembered* our appointment just in time.
    My friend *reminded* me of our appointment.

114. **respectably:** in a manner worthy of respect or esteem
    respectfully: with respect or honor, in ways that show high regard
    respectively: the items in the order indicated or named, separately
    Because he was wearing blue jeans, they told him he was not dressed *respectably* enough to enter the cathedral. His wife *respectfully* asked the bishop if he would change his mind.
    The project will require annual bonds of $150,000 and $250,000, *respectively*, in the next two years.

115. **restive:** refers to resistance to control
    restless: unable to rest
    People who live in dictatorial societies are usually *restive*.
    I spent a *restless* night; I got only three hours of sleep.

116. **resume** (*verb*): continue, take up again after an interruption
    résumé (*noun*): a summing up
    We will *resume* classes after the holiday.
    Katherine sent the director a *résumé* of her work experience.

117. **rout** (*verb*): defeat overwhelmingly
    route (*noun*): a fixed course
    Our football team *routed* the opponents 75 to 10.
    Her newspaper delivery *route* takes her past the hospital.

118. **say:** used with direct quotations and with indirect quotations when the person spoken to is not mentioned
    tell: used with indirect quotations when the person spoken to is mentioned
    Harry *said*, "When are you coming?"
    Doris *says* she is studying trigonometry.
    Doris *told* us she was studying trigonometry.

    Note these idiomatic uses of tell:
      tell the truth   tell a lie
      tell a story   tell time
      tell about something tell a secret
    Never use an indirect object after *say*; use *tell* instead:
      Tell me your name.

119. **sensual:** refers to the gratification of bodily pleasures
    sensuous: refers to the gratification of intellectual pleasures received through the senses
    The pornography aroused their *sensual* desires.
    There was a *sensuous* aroma in the air.

120. **set** (*transitive verb*): put or place in a specific spot
sit (*intransitive verb*): assume a resting position, remain
　　Set the plate on the table.
　　The plate now *sits* on the table.
　　First I *set* the chair on the porch, then I *sat* in it.

121. **some one**: an individual or a single unit (always followed by *of*)
someone: somebody, an unspecified person
　　No matter how hard we try to be careful, we usually lose *some one of*
　　　our books when we're at the beach.
　　I need *someone* to help me. Who will volunteer?

122. **some time**: some countable amount of time
sometime: an indefinite time
　　You'll need *some time* to work on your report. (some hours)
　　Come over to see us *sometime*, won't you?

123. **some times**: some specific times (days, weeks, etc.)
sometimes: now and then, occasionally
　　Some times are better than others for planting.
　　Sometimes we drive up to see the Leteliers.

124. **speak**: used with languages, greetings, and in formal settings
talk: refers to a conversation; often followed by an indirect object with *to*
　　Larissa *speaks* Tagalog and Mandarin Chinese.
　　The president will *speak* to our club.
　　Mrs. Mukabe *spoke* to her son about his sloppy attire.
　　It's not polite to *talk* during the professor's lecture.
　　She wanted to *talk to* me about her grades.

125. **stationary** (*adjective*): standing still, fixed
stationery (*noun*): writing paper and material
　　The stars appear *stationary*, but they're actually moving rapidly.
　　Melinda had her name printed on her *stationery*.

126. **statue**: a sculpted or carved likeness
stature: status, prestige; natural height
statute: a law
　　The *statue* of President Lincoln in the Memorial is enormous.
　　The governor had great *stature* in his state.
　　The soldier's *stature* (he was 6 feet, 6 inches tall) made him seem
　　　imposing.
　　The legislature passed a new *statute* limiting imports.

127. **sure** (*adjective*): certain, without doubt
surely (*adverb*): certainly, undoubtedly
　　I'm *sure* I can learn to drive that tractor.
　　Surely you're joking! It can't cost that much!

128. **tasteful:** showing or exhibiting good sense or judgment
tasty: delicious, flavorful
Her *tasteful* clothes contrasted with his gaudy ones.
This is a *tasty* stew; what's in it?

129. **than** (*conjunction*): used to introduce the second part of a comparison
then (*adverb*): next, at that time
Sheldon's hair is longer *than* his sister's.
We ate first, *then* we talked business.
In the 70's I lived in Senegal. I was much thinner *then than* I am now.

130. **their** (*possessive adjective*): belonging to them
there (*expletive or adverb*): in that place
they're: contraction for *they are*
There on the counter are *their* notebooks.
Do you have the qualifications *they're* asking for?

131. **threw** (*verb*): past tense of *throw* (toss, fling, hurl through the air)
through (*preposition*): from one side or end to the other
       (*adverb*): from beginning to end, completely
We just *threw* our old magazines away.
You have to go *through* Room 103 to get to the laboratory.
The customs agents examined our luggage *through* and *through*.

132. **to** (*preposition*): toward
too (*adverb*): in addition, also, more than enough
two (*adjective*): the sum of one + one
       (*noun*): the number after one
I have to hurry because I'm going *to* the airport.
I ate *too* much pie last night.
We're going now; do you want to go, *too*?
Two books.   One, *two*, three.

133. **tortuous:** twisting
torturous: causing pain or torture
The *tortuous* path led through the forest.
The cancer patient said that her pain was *torturous*.

134. **toward** is the correct term meaning "in the direction of." Never use
       towards.

135. **vice:** immoral behavior, evil practice
vise: a clamp
The police *vice* squad arrested six prostitutes.
We used a *vise* to hold the two parts together.

136. **waive:** relinquish, forgo
wave: move up and down or back and forth
The defendant *waived* his right to a jury trial, preferring instead to
    face the judge.
The flag *waved* in the wind.

137. **weather**: atmospheric conditions
    whether: in case, if, whichever one of two or more
      The *weather* has been cold lately.
      You are probably wondering *whether* the cold weather will affect our plans; it will not.

138. **who**: nominative case relative pronoun
    whom: objective case relative pronoun
      I asked the attendant *who* is wearing black to help us.
      The people *whom* Glynnis tutored returned to Italy.

139. **who's**: contraction for *who is*
    whose: possessive case of *who*
      Who's knocking at the door?
      Whose pen is this?

EXERCISES
(Answers are on page 210.)

A. Circle the word or words in parentheses that make the sentence correct.

   1. What (*percent, percentage*) of their GNP comes from the agricultural sector?

   2. My neighborhood is very (*quiet, quite*) at night.

   3. Professor Beame taught at the Sorbonne and at the University of California, Berkeley, in 1979 and 1980, (*respectfully, respectively*).

   4. Parents always teach their children to (*say, tell*) the truth.

   5. I think I'll be able to do that job (*some time, sometime*) next week.

   6. There is a marble (*statue, statute*) of Albert Einstein outside the science building.

   7. The exhibit of Incan artifacts was displayed very (*tastily, tastefully*).

   8. His grip was so strong that I felt as if I were in a (*vice, vise*).

   9. Do you think you'll (*accept, except*) his offer?

10. The U.S. Senate has the job of giving its (*advice, advise*) and consent to the President on Supreme Court appointments.

11. First we'll pick up our books at the bookstore, then (*after, afterward*) we'll register for classes.

12. Dana couldn't get his girl friend to agree (*to, with*) marry him.

13. This is the first time we've been (*all together, altogether*) in one place since 1975.

14. Justin said he didn't want to ski, and he didn't want to ice skate (*too, either*).

15. The (*amount, number*) of participants in our program has doubled.

16. The psychiatrist asked the patient to (*bare, bear*) her feelings.

17. Did you hear who (*beat, won*), Argentina or Italy?

18. When you behave in such a (*childish, childlike*) manner, I don't want to talk to you.

19. How does one convert British money into dollars and (*cents, scents*)?

20. Burlap is too (*coarse, course*) to use for clothing.

21. We've had (*continual, continuous*) sunshine for two weeks now.

22. The economists are currently (*devicing, devising*) a new plan to revitalize the economy.

23. Who (*does, makes*) breakfast in your house, you or your sister?

24. Try to answer (*every one, everyone*) of the questions.

25. At one time, Muhammed Ali was probably the most (*famous, infamous*) man in the world.

26. I see no other way to get into the car than to break the window (*forcefully, forcibly*).

27. The messenger of God went (*forth, fourth*) and spread The Word.

28. In olden times, criminals were (*hanged, hung*) in public executions.

29. Penny Peterson is teaching sign language to some baby (*gorillas, guerrillas*) in California.

30. I (*imply, infer*) from your remarks that you are a socialist.

B. For each of the words on the left, find its definition on the right. Then write the letter in the blank.

a. exceed	1. ＿＿＿ previously
b. assess	2. ＿＿＿ carry
c. effect	3. ＿＿＿ carried
d. already	4. ＿＿＿ complete
e. always	5. ＿＿＿ attorney
f. anyway	6. ＿＿＿ entirely
g. bear	7. ＿＿＿ surpass
h. borne	8. ＿＿＿ compassionate
i. capital	9. ＿＿＿ sum of money
j. sight	10. ＿＿＿ grow small
k. complement	11. ＿＿＿ result (noun)
l. counsel	12. ＿＿＿ scene
m. desert	13. ＿＿＿ basic truth
n. everyday	14. ＿＿＿ skeptical
o. formally	15. ＿＿＿ at all times
p. wholly	16. ＿＿＿ ceremoniously
q. humane	17. ＿＿＿ abandon
r. incredulous	18. ＿＿＿ evaluate
s. lessen	19. ＿＿＿ common
t. principle	20. ＿＿＿ nevertheless

C. In each of the following pairs of sentences, one sentence is correct and the other is incorrect because it misuses some term. Write the letter of the correct sentence in the space provided.

Example: (a) Remember me to call my mother.
(b) Remind me to call my mother. _____b_____

1. (a) This microcomputer is an ingenious device.
   (b) The designer of that rocket must be an ingenuous engineer. _____

2. (a) Many people were incredible when he first unfolded his plan.
   (b) Watching a caterpillar change into a butterfly is an incredible experience. _____

3. (a) I'm quitting today—this is my last cigarette.
   (b) Is that your latest cigarette, too? _____

4. (a) Let's be sure to learn Jason how to change diapers.
   (b) We'll have to teach Emma, too. _____

5. (a) The plurality of people in the United States speak English.
   (b) I now own 51 percent of the stock; I'm the majority stockholder. _____

6. (a) There are some critically ill patients in this clinic.
   (b) Dr. Schesser sees at least 25 patience a day. _____

7. (a) I wonder if Ramona passed the test.
   (b) We drove so fast that we past all the other cars. _____

8. (a) The sign said: "In case of fire, proceed to the nearest exit."
   (b) After finishing Part A, precede to Part B. _____

9. (a) The students rised their hands when the teacher asked the question.
   (b) Tomorrow the sun will rise at 6:52 A.M. _____

10. (a) The score was a real route, 100 to 49.
    (b) Which route should we take to get to the
        old mill near the river?   _____

D. Circle the word in parentheses that makes the sentence correct.

1. Does your family (*speak, talk*) English at home?

2. My father always (*set, sat*) in the same chair at the dinner
   table.

3. I bought my notebook at a (*stationary, stationery*) store.

4. Gretchen would rather play (*than, then*) study.

5. The pigeon flew (*threw, through*) the open window.

6. The (*weather, whether*) in Morocco is always pleasant.

7. Monday's (*addition, edition*) of *The New York Times* has
   several articles of interest.

8. (*Each, Every*) boy on the team worked toward winning the
   league championship.

9. Until you reminded me, I had forgotten our date (*altogether,
   all together*).

10. Dinner is (*almost, most*) ready; you'd better wash your hands.

11. Maggie and her sister are (*alumnae, alumni*) of the same
    college.

12. Jake will be here only (*as far as, until*) June.

13. (*Borrow, Lend*) me your pen for a moment, will you?

14. We plan to make a tent out of this old (*canvas, canvass*).

15. We (*compared, contrasted*) our coats and found that they
    were similar.

16. Danielle did such a (*credulous, creditable*) job of translating
    the document that they offered her a full-time job.

17. My goldfish (*died, dyed*) from lack of food.

18. I (*did, made*) the laundry this morning.

19. His treatise on the Middle East conflict showed (*incite, insight*) into the history of the region.

20. The town (*lies, lays*) at the foot of Bear Mountain.

ANSWER KEY

These exercises cover information presented in the section on usage that begins on **page 187.**

A.
1. percentage
2. quiet
3. respectively
4. tell
5. sometime
6. statue
7. tastefully
8. vise
9. accept
10. advice
11. afterward
12. to
13. all together
14. either
15. number
16. bare
17. won
18. childish
19. cents
20. coarse
21. continual
22. devising
23. makes
24. every one
25. famous
26. forcibly
27. forth
28. hanged
29. gorillas
30. infer

B.
1. *d*
2. *g*
3. *h*
4. *k*
5. *l*
6. *p*
7. *a*
8. *q*
9. *i*
10. *s*
11. *c*
12. *j*
13. *t*
14. *r*
15. *e*
16. *o*
17. *m*
18. *b*
19. *n*
20. *f*

C
1. *a*
2. *b*
3. *a*
4. *b*
5. *b*
6. *a*
7. *a*
8. *a*
9. *b*
10. *b*

D.
1. speak
2. sat
3. stationery
4. than
5. through
6. weather
7. edition
8. Every
9. altogether
10. almost
11. alumnae
12. until
13. Lend
14. canvas
15. compared
16. creditable
17. died
18. did
19. insight
20. lies

SAMPLE TEST 1

Sample Test 1—Answer Sheet

When you have chosen your answer to any question, blacken the corresponding space on the answer sheet below. Make sure your marking completely fills the answer space. If you change an answer, erase the previous marking completely.

For convenience, you may wish to remove this sheet from the book and keep it in front of you during the test.

1 Ⓐ Ⓑ Ⓒ Ⓓ	11 Ⓐ Ⓑ Ⓒ Ⓓ	21 Ⓐ Ⓑ Ⓒ Ⓓ	31 Ⓐ Ⓑ Ⓒ Ⓓ
2 Ⓐ Ⓑ Ⓒ Ⓓ	12 Ⓐ Ⓑ Ⓒ Ⓓ	22 Ⓐ Ⓑ Ⓒ Ⓓ	32 Ⓐ Ⓑ Ⓒ Ⓓ
3 Ⓐ Ⓑ Ⓒ Ⓓ	13 Ⓐ Ⓑ Ⓒ Ⓓ	23 Ⓐ Ⓑ Ⓒ Ⓓ	33 Ⓐ Ⓑ Ⓒ Ⓓ
4 Ⓐ Ⓑ Ⓒ Ⓓ	14 Ⓐ Ⓑ Ⓒ Ⓓ	24 Ⓐ Ⓑ Ⓒ Ⓓ	34 Ⓐ Ⓑ Ⓒ Ⓓ
5 Ⓐ Ⓑ Ⓒ Ⓓ	15 Ⓐ Ⓑ Ⓒ Ⓓ	25 Ⓐ Ⓑ Ⓒ Ⓓ	35 Ⓐ Ⓑ Ⓒ Ⓓ
6 Ⓐ Ⓑ Ⓒ Ⓓ	16 Ⓐ Ⓑ Ⓒ Ⓓ	26 Ⓐ Ⓑ Ⓒ Ⓓ	36 Ⓐ Ⓑ Ⓒ Ⓓ
7 Ⓐ Ⓑ Ⓒ Ⓓ	17 Ⓐ Ⓑ Ⓒ Ⓓ	27 Ⓐ Ⓑ Ⓒ Ⓓ	37 Ⓐ Ⓑ Ⓒ Ⓓ
8 Ⓐ Ⓑ Ⓒ Ⓓ	18 Ⓐ Ⓑ Ⓒ Ⓓ	28 Ⓐ Ⓑ Ⓒ Ⓓ	38 Ⓐ Ⓑ Ⓒ Ⓓ
9 Ⓐ Ⓑ Ⓒ Ⓓ	19 Ⓐ Ⓑ Ⓒ Ⓓ	29 Ⓐ Ⓑ Ⓒ Ⓓ	39 Ⓐ Ⓑ Ⓒ Ⓓ
10 Ⓐ Ⓑ Ⓒ Ⓓ	20 Ⓐ Ⓑ Ⓒ Ⓓ	30 Ⓐ Ⓑ Ⓒ Ⓓ	40 Ⓐ Ⓑ Ⓒ Ⓓ

40 questions
25 minutes

Sample Test 1

An answer key for this test is on page 221. Explanatory answers begin on page 221.

PART A (15 questions; 10 minutes)

In part A each problem consists of an incomplete sentence. Four words or phrases, marked (*a*), (*b*), (*c*), (*d*), are given beneath the sentence. You are to choose the one word or phrase that best completes the sentence. Then on your answer sheet, find the number of the problem and mark your answer.

1. I haven't seen you in years; do you _____ play the clarinet?

   (*a*) yet
   (*b*) still
   (*c*) already
   (*d*) anymore

2. We were surprised when we found out that it was _____ than anyone had predicted.

   (*a*) as cold
   (*b*) colder
   (*c*) more cold
   (*d*) cold

3. Mr. Douglas has been waiting to see Mr. Forchik _____ .

   (*a*) for three hours ago
   (*b*) since three hours
   (*c*) since noon
   (*d*) since three hours ago

4. Their office is located _____ 1811 Wynnewood Road _____ Philadelphia, but she's _____ New Jersey.

   (*a*) on . . . at . . . from
   (*b*) at . . . in . . . from
   (*c*) in . . . on . . . by
   (*d*) on . . . in . . . at

5. Summer in the Northwest means _____

    (a) when it doesn't rain for a week.
    (b) where it doesn't rain for a week.
    (c) if it doesn't rain for a week.
    (d) a week with no rain.

6. We decided that _____ them ski was preferable to skiing ourselves.

    (a) to watch
    (b) watching
    (c) watch
    (d) to watching

7. _____ my keys on that table; please lock the door on your way out.

    (a) There is
    (b) There are
    (c) Here is
    (d) Here are

8. The nurse reported that on her floor _____ .

    (a) the nurses use a lot of tape
    (b) they use a lot of tape
    (c) a lot of tape is used
    (d) they use plenty of tape

9. Joyce said, _____

    (a) Where is the restaurant.
    (b) Where is the restaurant?
    (c) "Where is the restaurant?"
    (d) "Where is the restaurant."

10. Mr. Goldfarb will be able to see us early today, _____?

    (a) can't he
    (b) no
    (c) won't he
    (d) will he

11. They'll probably _____ the national anthem by the time you get there.

    (a) are playing
    (b) playing
    (c) be playing
    (d) play

12. I thought I was dialing Sybil's number, but I was actually dialing _____

   (a) Aubrey.
   (b) Aubreys.
   (c) Aubrey's.
   (d) of Aubrey.

13. Ted recommended that they reward _____ by taking the rest of the day off.

   (a) themself
   (b) theirselves
   (c) theirself
   (d) themselves

14. _____ asked _____ to water his plants while he was away.

   (a) Him . . . her
   (b) He . . . her
   (c) He . . . she
   (d) He . . . his

15. She is a much better sailor _____ he.

   (a) as
   (b) like
   (c) than
   (d) from

PART B (25 questions; 15 minutes)

   Each problem in Part B consists of a sentence in which four words or phrases are underlined. The four underlined parts of the sentence are marked (a), (b), (c), (d). You are to identify the one underlined word or phrase that should be corrected or rewritten. Then on your answer sheet, find the number of the problem and mark your answer.

16. Forty feet of dock space are a lot for a boat the size of yours,
    _____   _____   _____
       a   b   c
    don't you think?
    _____
       d

17. The number of attornies in Samuelson's office has risen from
                    _____   _____   _____
                       a   b   c
    from 5 to 10.
    _____
       d

18. The nurse asked <u>me and Bonnie</u> <u>to leave</u> the room <u>while</u> she
        a   *b*   *c*

 <u>gave</u> Eleanor a sponge bath.
 d

19. I didn't <u>see</u> the omens <u>until</u> too late; I <u>ought to see</u> them
    a   *b*   *c*

 <u>earlier</u>.
 d

20. Rolf didn't sleep <u>well</u> <u>because</u> of <u>the</u> thunder, and his wife
       a *b*   *c*

 <u>didn't neither</u>.
 d

21. We'll <u>have to</u> <u>wait</u> for Shelly; she's the only one of us <u>who</u>
    a   *b*   *c*

 <u>know</u> what the candidate looks like.
 d

22. <u>Most</u> <u>of</u> the sugar <u>in</u> the green canister <u>were covered</u> with
  a *b*   *c*   *d*

 mold.

23. Surprise! It's been <u>me</u> all the time! I <u>was just disguising</u> <u>my</u>
       a   *b*   *c*

 voice <u>to fool</u> you.
   d

24. Our files—<u>carefully and personally</u> designed by Ms. Daltrey
         a

 —<u>has</u> <u>become</u> popular in other branches <u>as well as</u> ours.
   b *c*   *d*

25. If I were you, and, with <u>very little</u> preplanning or notice,
           a

 <u>was able</u> to move, <u>I'd</u> do <u>it</u>.
  b   *c* *d*

26. When she was enrolled <u>at</u> UMBC (I think it was in the <u>late</u>
         a   *b*

 1970's), she <u>has studied</u> <u>the</u> biological sciences.
      c   *d*

27. She asked, "Cant you see the trouble you're causing?"
          _a_   _b_   _c_   _d_

28. No one has said anything yet, but I think I might be getting
              _a_   _b_   _c_   _d_
    my promotion next month.

29. Marlene Elbin didn't finish the yoga course and I did.
                  _a_   _b_   _c_   _d_

30. I had supposed to go to Iran to work a few years ago, but,
              _a_   _b_   _c_
    of course, I changed my plans.
      _d_

31. I have no objection to Marie riding with us to work
       _a_   _b_   _c_
    in the morning.
       _d_

32. Mr. Vermiel excitedly ran up to his nephew and said, "I'm
                       _a_   _b_
    sure glad to see you, Steve."
     _c_   _d_

33. The blades on this lawn mower are the most dullest of any
     _a_   _b_   _c_
    I've ever seen.
      _d_

34. Pete Rose was quoted as saying that despite that his team
            _a_   _b_
    lost, he would continue to play baseball.
       _c_   _d_

35. We arrived after they; we hoped that no one would notice our
     _a_   _b_   _c_   _d_
    lateness.

36. We are thinking of either spending Thanksgiving or Christ-
       _a_   _b_
    mas with my in-laws in Florida.
       _c_   _d_

37. I put <u>the</u> stew we <u>are going</u> <u>to eat</u> <u>on the stove.</u>
          a   *b*   *c*   *d*

38. The time I love <u>to remember</u> <u>are</u> our several visits to <u>Sylvia's</u>
                  a   *b*   *c*
retreat <u>in</u> the Adirondacks.
      d

39. <u>The</u> scoutmaster warned <u>his</u> charges in <u>a</u> stern voice
    a   *b*   *c*
<u>don't swim</u> in the lake.
     d

40. <u>Oops!</u> I think I <u>did a mistake</u> on that <u>mid-term</u> exam in
    a   *b*   *c*
<u>organic chemistry.</u>
       d

STOP! End of Sample Test 1

Sample Test 1: Answer Key

1. *b*	11. *c*	21. *d*	31. *b*
2. *b*	12. *c*	22. *d*	32. *c*
3. *c*	13. *d*	23. *a*	33. *b*
4. *b*	14. *b*	24. *b*	34. *b*
5. *d*	15. *c*	25. *b*	35. *b*
6. *b*	16. *b*	26. *c*	36. *b*
7. *b*	17. *a*	27. *b*	37. *d*
8. *a*	18. *a*	28. *d*	38. *b*
9. *c*	19. *c*	29. *c*	39. *d*
10. *c*	20. *d*	30. *a*	40. *b*

Sample Test 1: Explanatory Answers

The numbers in parentheses refer to the rules covering each point.

1. (*b*) By definition and usage, only (*b*) is acceptable in this context and construction because *still* expresses continuous action up to the present. *Yet* occurs at the end of a question; *already* means "previously"; *anymore* occurs at the end of a question and indicates something no longer happening. (**139; 141**)

2. (*b*) Only (*b*) is acceptable; the comparison is of a one-syllable adjective. Choice (*a*) is an inappropriate type of comparison; (*c*) and (*d*) are unacceptable forms for comparison. (**157; 160; 169*u***)

3. (*c*) Only (*c*) is an acceptable English phrase. (**188**)

4. (*b*) Choice (*b*) uses the appropriate prepositions for this construction; *at* for a specific address; *in* for a city; and *from* to indicate a person's place of birth. (**190*f*; 190*g***)

5. (*d*) Only (*d*) is acceptable as a noun phrase, which is called for by the construction of the sentence (Summer means *what*?). The other choices are either adjectival or adverbial phrases/clauses. (**133; 212**)

6. (*b*) Only (*b*) is a gerund, which properly parallels the other gerund (*skiing*) in the comparison. Choice (*a*) is an infinitive; (*c*) and (*d*) are grammatically unacceptable. (**231**)

7. (*b*) Only (*b*) is acceptable. *Keys* is a plural subject that requires a plural predicate (*are*); the phrase "on that table" indicates that the keys are not *here* but *there*. (**202; 237**)

8. (a) Only (a) is clear and direct. Choices (b) and (d) have vague pronoun references (*they*); (c) shifts needlessly to passive voice. **(252)**

9. (c) Only (c) uses punctuation properly. A direct quote uses quotation marks, and questions conclude with question marks. **(288; 291)**

10. (c) Only (c) is an acceptable tag ending for this sentence; it uses the same auxiliary verb and changes the affirmative to negative. None of the other choices fill these requirements for tag questions. **(94)**

11. (c) Only (c) correctly uses the future progressive tense, expressing that some event will be occurring in the future when another event occurs. **(83)**

12. (c) Only (c) is acceptable; a possessive form (*'s*) is used even when the noun is not expressed. Thus, "... I was actually dialing Aubrey's (number)." Choice (a) compares a number with a person; (b) has no apostrophe; (d) is grammatically unacceptable. **(19)**

13. (d) Only (d) is acceptable as a recognized reflexive. Choices (a), (b), and (c) are all grammatically unacceptable in any circumstance. **(25)**

14. (b) Only (b) uses the correct cases. A nominative case pronoun is required as the subject of the verb, and an objective case pronoun is needed as the indirect object of the same verb. **(41; 43b)**

15. (c) Only (c) is acceptable; *than*, a conjunction, introduces the second element in a comparison. Choice (a) is also a conjunction, but is inappropriate in this construction; (b) is a verb or preposition; (d) is a preposition. **(45)**

16. (b) The feet are not being thought of individually, but rather as a whole unit; thus, the term is a singular subject that requires a singular predicate. Thus, "Forty feet of space is a lot ...." **(2a; 239)**

17. (a) Spelling error; it should be *attorneys*. **(8a)**

18. (a) In compound constructions, the personal pronoun should be last. Thus, "The nurse asked Bonnie and me to leave. ..." **(24)**

19. (c) "*Ought to have*" + the past participle is the auxiliary that indicates past necessity. Thus, "... late; I ought to have seen them earlier." **(112)**

20. (d) The connection of negative statements that are in agreement requires different phrasing: "... and his wife didn't either" or "... and neither did his wife." **(97)**

21. (d) The antecedent of *who* is *she*, not *us*; therefore, the relative pronoun is singular, and its verb must be singular. Thus, "... she's the only one of us who knows what the ...." **(32; 248)**

22. (d) When *most* (or any other indefinite pronoun) is used as a subject, look to the meaning to determine whether it is singular or plural. In this sentence, *most* refers to a noncountable noun, a whole; the sugar in the canister is considered as one unit, not as individual granules. Therefore, the subject is singular and requires a singular predicate. Thus, "Most of the sugar . . . was covered with mold." (38; 250)

23. (a) Even though this structure would be acceptable in informal speech, it is incorrect in formal, written English. The verb *be* requires a predicate nominative; therefore, the pronoun must be nominative case. Thus, "It's been I all the time!" (41)

24. (b) *Files* is a plural subject that requires a plural predicate. Thus, "Our files . . . have become popular . . . ." (50; 234)

25. (b) The mood of the verb is subjunctive ("If I were you . . . ."); therefore, the second part of the compound verb must also be in the subjunctive mood. Thus, "If I were you, . . . were able to move, ..." (68)

26. (c) The dependent clause that opens the sentence sets the scene in the past tense; indeed, there was a beginning and an end to the past time of enrollment at the university. The main clause verb, therefore, cannot reflect continued-up-to-the-present time as it does in this present perfect tense. The main clause verb must also be in the past tense. Thus, "When she was enrolled . . . she studied the biological sciences." (78)

27. (b) The correct contraction for *can not* is *can't*. (91; 258)

28. (d) When the present tense of such verbs as *think, say, tell, etc.,* is used, then the present tense of *may, can, shall,* and *will* is used. When the past tense is used, then *might, could, should,* and *would* are used. Thus, ". . . but I think I may be getting . . . ." (92)

29. (c) Since the two thoughts are contrasting or contradictory, the appropriate connective is *but*. Thus, ". . . didn't finish . . . but I did." (96)

30. (a) The correct form of the auxiliary verb that expresses expectation or anticipation is *be supposed to* + the simple form of the verb; thus, "I was supposed to go to Iran . . . ." (109)

31. (b) *Riding* is a gerund modified by a proper noun that is possessive case. It's the *riding* that the speaker has no objection to. Thus, "I have no objection to Marie's riding with us . . . ." (17; 124)

32. (c) *Sure* is an adjective meaning "certain." Since *glad* is also an adjective, the word modifying it should be an adverb. Thus, "I'm surely glad to see you, Steve." or "I'm certainly glad to see you, Steve." (146)

33. (b) Short adjectives form their superlative degrees by adding *-est*, not *most*. Thus, "... are the dullest of any ...." (**161; 163**)

34. (b) *Despite* should be followed by a noun. When a clause follows, the term should change to *despite the fact that*. Thus, "... as saying that despite the fact that his team lost, he would continue ...." (**184**)

35. (b) Since *after* is used as a preposition in this sentence, its pronoun object must be objective case. Thus, "We arrived after them; we hoped ...." *After*, used as a conjunction, would be acceptable in this construction: "We arrived after they did; we hoped ...." (**192**)

36. (b) *Either* is misplaced. As part of the correlative conjunction *either ... or*, it must be placed in such a way that the two parts correlate items of equal rank, namely, the two holidays. Thus, "We are thinking of spending either Thanksgiving or Christmas with ...." (**199**)

37. (d) This phrase is misplaced. One might wonder if we are going to be on the stove when we eat the stew. The placement of modifying elements is important to sentence sense. Thus, "I just started to cook the stew we're going to eat. It's on the stove." (**219**)

38. (b) A singular subject (*time*) requires a singular verb even when the predicate nominative is different in number. Thus, "The time I love to remember is our several visits ...." (**238**)

39. (d) Commands should be expressed by an infinitive when they are quoted indirectly. Thus, " ... in a stern voice not to swim in the lake." When the command is quoted directly, quotation marks are needed: "... in a stern voice, 'Don't swim in the lake.'" A *charge* is a person or thing entrusted to the care of another. (**256**)

40. (b) The correct usage here is *make a mistake*. Thus, "Oops! I think I made a mistake on that mid-term ...." (Usage **61**)

SAMPLE TEST 2

Sample Test 2—Answer Sheet

When you have chosen your answer to any question, blacken the corresponding space on the answer sheet below. Make sure your marking completely fills the answer space. If you change an answer, erase the previous marking completely.

For convenience, you may wish to remove this sheet from the book and keep it in front of you during the test.

1 Ⓐ Ⓑ Ⓒ Ⓓ	11 Ⓐ Ⓑ Ⓒ Ⓓ	21 Ⓐ Ⓑ Ⓒ Ⓓ	31 Ⓐ Ⓑ Ⓒ Ⓓ
2 Ⓐ Ⓑ Ⓒ Ⓓ	12 Ⓐ Ⓑ Ⓒ Ⓓ	22 Ⓐ Ⓑ Ⓒ Ⓓ	32 Ⓐ Ⓑ Ⓒ Ⓓ
3 Ⓐ Ⓑ Ⓒ Ⓓ	13 Ⓐ Ⓑ Ⓒ Ⓓ	23 Ⓐ Ⓑ Ⓒ Ⓓ	33 Ⓐ Ⓑ Ⓒ Ⓓ
4 Ⓐ Ⓑ Ⓒ Ⓓ	14 Ⓐ Ⓑ Ⓒ Ⓓ	24 Ⓐ Ⓑ Ⓒ Ⓓ	34 Ⓐ Ⓑ Ⓒ Ⓓ
5 Ⓐ Ⓑ Ⓒ Ⓓ	15 Ⓐ Ⓑ Ⓒ Ⓓ	25 Ⓐ Ⓑ Ⓒ Ⓓ	35 Ⓐ Ⓑ Ⓒ Ⓓ
6 Ⓐ Ⓑ Ⓒ Ⓓ	16 Ⓐ Ⓑ Ⓒ Ⓓ	26 Ⓐ Ⓑ Ⓒ Ⓓ	36 Ⓐ Ⓑ Ⓒ Ⓓ
7 Ⓐ Ⓑ Ⓒ Ⓓ	17 Ⓐ Ⓑ Ⓒ Ⓓ	27 Ⓐ Ⓑ Ⓒ Ⓓ	37 Ⓐ Ⓑ Ⓒ Ⓓ
8 Ⓐ Ⓑ Ⓒ Ⓓ	18 Ⓐ Ⓑ Ⓒ Ⓓ	28 Ⓐ Ⓑ Ⓒ Ⓓ	38 Ⓐ Ⓑ Ⓒ Ⓓ
9 Ⓐ Ⓑ Ⓒ Ⓓ	19 Ⓐ Ⓑ Ⓒ Ⓓ	29 Ⓐ Ⓑ Ⓒ Ⓓ	39 Ⓐ Ⓑ Ⓒ Ⓓ
10 Ⓐ Ⓑ Ⓒ Ⓓ	20 Ⓐ Ⓑ Ⓒ Ⓓ	30 Ⓐ Ⓑ Ⓒ Ⓓ	40 Ⓐ Ⓑ Ⓒ Ⓓ

Sample Test 2

An answer key for this test is on page 235. Explanatory answers begin on page 235.

PART A (15 questions; 10 minutes)

In Part A each problem consists of an incomplete sentence. Four words or phrases, marked (*a*), (*b*), (*c*), (*d*), are given beneath each sentence. You are to choose the one word or phrase that best completes the sentence. Then on your answer sheet, find the number of the problem and mark your answer.

1. Admiral Rickover is the expert _____ the committee wants to subpoena.

   (*a*) who
   (*b*) whom
   (*c*) that
   (*d*) whose

2. Will you please _____ what time it is.

   (*a*) say me
   (*b*) tell me
   (*c*) say
   (*d*) tell

3. We _____ my relatives in Baltimore _____.

   (*a*) often on weekends . . . visit
   (*b*) on weekends . . . often visit
   (*c*) often visit . . . on weekends
   (*d*) visit . . . on weekends often

4. The Atacama Desert is one of _____ places on earth.

   (*a*) the most desolatest
   (*b*) most desolate
   (*c*) the desolatest
   (*d*) the most desolate

5. My philodendron has responded well to this new house plant fertilizer, has _____ ?

    (a) yours
    (b) your's
    (c) yours'
    (d) the yours

6. Let's not allow this news to leak out; let's keep it _____ the three of us.

    (a) by
    (b) of
    (c) among
    (d) between

7. The _____ of the new administration produced nothing of historical consequence.

    (a) first 100 days
    (b) 100 first days
    (c) first days of 100
    (d) 100-first days

8. When I told Maggie that I loved volleyball, she said,

    (a) "I am too."
    (b) "So can I."
    (c) "So do I."
    (d) "I don't either."

9. The sign was put there _____ people to wear hard hats in this area.

    (a) reminding
    (b) to remind
    (c) that reminds
    (d) for reminding

10. This isn't my jacket, it's my _____ .

    (a) father's-in-law
    (b) father in law's
    (c) father's in law
    (d) father-in-law's

11. She said, "I was just sitting here waiting for you." Then she explained that she _____ to talk to me.

   (a) was just hoping
   (b) had been hoping
   (c) has been hoping
   (d) hoped

12. She seated us, poured the tea, served the scones, _____

   (a) and the candles.
   (b) lit the candles.
   (c) and lit the candles.
   (d) and she lit the candles.

13. She said that when he was ready, he'd nod at his two helpers, namely, _____

   (a) he and she.
   (b) he and her.
   (c) him and her.
   (d) him and she.

14. Yesterday, in an old bookstore, I came _____ an 1866 edition of *Uncle Tom's Cabin*.

   (a) across
   (b) back
   (c) out of
   (d) from

15. _____ you _____ to see my notes on the physics lecture?

   (a) Will . . . like
   (b) Could . . . like
   (c) Should . . . like
   (d) Would . . . like

PART B (25 questions; 15 minutes)

Each problem in Part B consists of a sentence in which four words or phrases are underlined. The four underlined parts of the sentence are marked (a), (b), (c), (d). You are to identify the one underlined word or phrase that should be corrected or rewritten. Then on your answer sheet, find the number of the problem and mark your answer.

16. Eighty-five percent of the beds in that hospital is usually
    _____   ____   __ _____
         a   b   c   d
    filled.

17. She was so excited, our niece, she fell coming to greet us.
             __ _____   _____ _____
             a   b   c   d

18. Taking a long walk in the woods is a perfect way to put your
    _____   __   _____
      a   b   c
    every day cares behind you.
    _____
        d

19. I won't lend my brother my snowplow because I am afraid if
            ____   __
             a   b
    he will forget to return it.
                    _____ __
                        c   d

20. The 7 pm news, with full-color action shots of the assassina-
        _____   _____
            a   b
    tion attempt, is coming on now.
                  _____ ___
                       c   d

21. Chicago is clearly the largest of all the cities in the midwest.
               _____ _____   __   _____
                  a   b   c   d

22. Is any of the glass figurines on display in that case valuable?
    __ ___   __   __
    a   b   c   d

23. They don't use oxes for heavy work anymore; they use water
         _____ ____   _____
            a   b c   d
    buffalo.

24. I can't get WAJM on this set; they must be gone off the air.
      _____   __   _____ _____
          a   b   c   d

25. Claude and Sara were annoyed by their guest forgetting to
                       _____   _____ _____ _____
                            a   b   c   d
    turn off the water in the bathroom.

26. We parked <u>in front of</u> the U.N. building <u>so that</u> we <u>saw</u> the
              a   *b*   *c*
Yugoslav delegation <u>arrive</u>.
                   d

27. The pilot <u>we met</u> in the coffee shop is the one <u>which</u> <u>flew</u> the
           a   *b*   *c*
747 we <u>arrived on</u>.
         d

28. <u>Every</u> book, magazine, and pamphlet in this library
   a
<u>are being readied for</u> a new system <u>of</u> <u>cataloging</u>.
        b   *c*   *d*

29. <u>If</u> the procedures seem complex <u>at first</u>, just relax and <u>do</u>
   a   *b*   *c*
them like <u>I</u>.
        d

30. We'll be able <u>to leave</u> <u>as soon as</u> Dr. Chamberlin <u>will turn off</u>
               a   *b*   *c*
<u>all</u> the etna burners.
 d

31. The grease <u>monkey</u> <u>was changed</u> my oil filter when I called
           a   *b*
<u>to ask</u> when the car would be <u>ready</u>.
   c   *d*

32. Walter Payton was the player <u>who</u> we <u>cheered</u> <u>on</u> <u>that</u> last
                          a   *b*   *c* *d*
play.

33. <u>If</u> you get your house <u>paint</u> by that painter, <u>be sure</u> <u>to get</u> a
   a   *b*   *c*   *d*
guarantee.

34. <u>The</u> promoters <u>teach</u> the beauty queen contestants to
   a   *b*
<u>radiantly</u> walk <u>down</u> the runway.
     c   *d*

35. For the <u>past year</u> we <u>have been considering</u> <u>to buy</u> a small
     a   *b*   *c*

 <u>chalet</u> in the mountains.
  d

36. We barely <u>didn't get</u> to the store <u>before</u> <u>its</u> 10 P.M. <u>closing</u>
     a   *b* *c*   *d*

 time.

37. We drive <u>occasionally</u> to the beach, <u>where</u> my aunt <u>has</u> a
     a   *b*   *c*

 <u>year-round</u> apartment.
  d

38. Patrolman Hawkins is <u>a</u> <u>better</u> shot <u>than</u> <u>anyone</u> in the
         a *b*   *c* *d*

 Plainfield Police Department.

39. I looked <u>up</u> the answer <u>to</u> your question, and according <u>with</u>
    a   *b*   *c*

 the encyclopedia, Skye is an island <u>off</u> Scotland.
             d

40. The official record <u>shows</u> that <u>all</u> of the people did not want
       a   *b*

 <u>Ms.</u> Abzug as <u>their</u> leader.
  c   *d*

STOP! End of Sample Test 2

Sample Test 2: Answer Key

1. *b*	11. *b*	21. *d*	31. *b*
2. *b*	12. *c*	22. *a*	32. *a*
3. *c*	13. *c*	23. *b*	33. *b*
4. *d*	14. *a*	24. *c*	34. *c*
5. *a*	15. *d*	25. *c*	35. *c*
6. *c*	16. *c*	26. *c*	36. *a*
7. *a*	17. *b*	27. *b*	37. *a*
8. *c*	18. *d*	28. *b*	38. *d*
9. *b*	19. *b*	29. *d*	39. *c*
10. *d*	20. *a*	30. *c*	40. *b*

Sample Test 2: Explanatory Answers

The numbers in parentheses refer to the rules covering each point.

1. (*b*) Only (*b*) is acceptable; an objective case pronoun is required as the object of the infinitive *to subpoena*. Choice (*a*) is nominative case; (*c*) is not used to refer to specific people; (*d*) is possessive. (**30; 120**)

2. (*b*) Only (*b*) is acceptable; *tell*, with an indirect object, is used with this type of construction. (Usage **118**)

3. (*c*) Only (*c*) uses the appropriate word order: adverbs of frequency, main verbs, then adverbs of time. (**154; 155**)

4. (*d*) Only (*d*) uses the correct form of the superlative degree of comparison; the other three choices are grammatically unacceptable in any circumstance. (**162; 163; 164**)

5. (*a*) Only (*a*) is grammatically acceptable. Possessive personal pronouns never use apostrophes. (**42**)

6. (*c*) Choice (*c*) grammatically expresses in the midst of more than two people; the other prepositions are unacceptable in this context. Choice (*d*) would be acceptable if there were only two people. (**180**)

7. (*a*) Only (*a*) is acceptable; the words *first* and *last* precede numbers and do not use hyphens. (**150**)

8. (*c*) Only (*c*) is an acceptable rejoinder in this sentence; choices (*a*) and (*b*) use the wrong auxiliary; (*d*) expresses inappropriate negation. (**98**)

9. (*b*) Only (*b*) is acceptable; the infinitive is used to express purpose. (**127**)

10. (*d*) Only (*d*) follows correct rules of punctuation. Compound nouns that function with the force of one word require hyphens; possessives use apostrophes after the last term even when the noun is understood. Thus, ". . . my father-in-law's (jacket)." (**15; 19; 282**)

11. (*b*) Only (*b*) uses the correct tense. When going from direct to indirect discourse, the past progressive changes to the past perfect progressive. (**253***d*)

12. (*c*) Only (*c*) is acceptable. The pattern "verb + *the* + object" is completed by using *and* before the last item. Choice (*a*) has no verb; (*b*) has no *and*; (*d*) needlessly repeats *she*. (**229**)

13. (*c*) Only (*c*) is acceptable. The two pronouns are in opposition to a noun (*helpers*) that is the object of the preposition *at*; thus, both pronouns must be objective case. The other choices have at least one pronoun in nominative case. (**44; 201**)

14. (*a*) By definition, (*a*) means "to discover by accident," which is the intended meaning of the sentence. Choice (*b*) means "return"; (*c*) means "emerge from"; (*d*) means "originate in." (**191**)

15. (*d*) Only (*d*) is acceptable. The auxiliary *would like* with an infinitive is an expression used to indicate an invitation. None of the other choices are acceptable English expressions. (**110**)

16. (*c*) *Beds* is a plural noun that governs the subject and makes it plural; therefore, the verb should be plural. Thus, "Eighty-five percent of the beds in that hospital are usually filled." (**240**)

17. (*b*) This is a misused appositive. Appositives must follow their nouns or pronouns directly. There is also redundant use of a pronoun. The correct answer would be "Our niece was so excited, she fell . . . ." (**23; 200; 201**)

18. (*d*) *Every day* is an adverb meaning "each single day." *Everyday* is an adjective meaning "daily" or "common." An adjective is needed to modify the noun *cares*: ". . . put your everyday cares behind you." (Usage **64**)

19. (*b*) *If* means "in the event that"; in this sentence it is an inappropriate word. The correct answer would read: ". . . because I am afraid that he will forget . . . ." (**226**)

20. (*a*) The correct abbreviation for time after noon is *P.M.*: "The 7 P.M. news . . . ." (Abbreviations)

21. (*d*) The *Midwest*, a specified region of the country, must be capitalized: ". . . cities in the Midwest." Note that when this word is used as a general direction, it is not capitalized: "That city is in the midwestern part of the state." (**301**)

22. (*a*) *Any* is a plural indefinite pronoun when it is used with a countable noun (*figurines*); thus, as a plural subject, it requires a plural verb: "Are any of the glass figurines . . . ." **(38; 250)**

23. (*b*) Improper plural; it should be *oxen*. **(11d)**

24. (*c*) *Must have* + the past participle is the auxiliary that expresses high probability about past or future occurrences. Thus, ". . . they must have gone off the air." **(105)**

25. (*c*) When gerunds are preceded by nouns in the possessive case, those nouns should use apostrophes. Thus, ". . . were annoyed by their guest's forgetting to . . . ." **(17)**

26. (*c*) The tense of the verb is correct, but the phrase *so that* must be linked with *can, will,* or *may* in order to express reason or cause. Thus, ". . . so that we could see the Yugoslav . . . ." **(101)**

27. (*b*) The relative pronoun *which* may be used to refer to specific animals or things, but not people. *Who, whom,* and *whose,* in their respective cases, refer to specific people. Thus, ". . . is the one who flew the 747 . . . ." **(30)**

28. (*b*) When *every* modifies a subject, the predicate is singular. Thus, "Every book . . . in this library is being readied . . . ." **(36)**

29. (*d*) Since *like* is a preposition, its pronoun object must be objective case: ". . . just relax and do them like me." This sentence could be restructured to use a conjunction, in which case it would read: ". . . just relax and do them as I do." **(45)**

30. (*c*) In subjunctive mood sentences, the present tense is used to indicate a future event: ". . . as soon as Dr. Chamberlin turns off all the . . . ." **(66)**

31. (*b*) Since the changing of the oil filter was beginning at the same time that another past event was occurring (*I called*), the appropriate tense is past progressive. Thus, "The grease monkey was changing my oil filter . . . ." *Grease monkey* is a slang term for a gas station employee. **(82)**

32. (*a*) In the dependent clause, the relative pronoun (which also introduces the clause) is the direct object of the verb *cheered*; thus, the pronoun must be objective case: ". . . was the player whom we cheered . . . ." **(53)**

33. (*b*) The correct form of the auxiliary that indicates the cause of some event is *get* + the past participle. Thus, "If you get your house painted by that painter . . . ." **(104)**

34. (*c*) There is no reason to split the infinitive *to walk* with this adverb. The sentence should read: ". . . contestants to walk down the runway radiantly." **(121)**

35. (c) When *consider* is followed by a verbal, it must be a gerund. Thus, "... we have been considering buying a small chalet ...." A *chalet* is a country home with a wide, heavy roof. (125)

36. (a) The adverb *barely*, which means "by a very little," gives the sentence its negative form; thus, no other negation should be used. Thus, "We barely got to the store ...." (132; 211)

37. (a) Adverbs of frequency should be placed before main verbs. Thus, "Occasionally we drive to the beach ...." or "We occasionally drive to the beach ...." The term *year-round* means continuous throughout the year, in all seasons. (155)

38. (d) Since Hawkins is also a member of the Police Department, a construction that compares him with a group that includes him is inappropriate. Use language that does not compare him with himself: "... a better shot than anyone else in the ...." (167)

39. (c) The correct preposition for this verb, which means "on the authority of," is *to*: "... and according to the encyclopedia ...." (191)

40. (b) This construction seems to say that no one wanted her to be the leader. The meaning is probably that some people wanted her and some didn't. It would be better to reword the sentence for the sake of logic, as follows: "The official record shows that not all of the people wanted Ms. Abzug as their leader." (Usage 11)

SAMPLE TEST 3

Sample Test 3—Answer Sheet

When you have chosen your answer to any question, blacken the corresponding space on the answer sheet below. Make sure your marking completely fills the answer space. If you change an answer, erase the previous marking completely.

For convenience, you may wish to remove this sheet from the book and keep it in front of you during the test.

1 Ⓐ Ⓑ Ⓒ Ⓓ	11 Ⓐ Ⓑ Ⓒ Ⓓ	21 Ⓐ Ⓑ Ⓒ Ⓓ	31 Ⓐ Ⓑ Ⓒ Ⓓ
2 Ⓐ Ⓑ Ⓒ Ⓓ	12 Ⓐ Ⓑ Ⓒ Ⓓ	22 Ⓐ Ⓑ Ⓒ Ⓓ	32 Ⓐ Ⓑ Ⓒ Ⓓ
3 Ⓐ Ⓑ Ⓒ Ⓓ	13 Ⓐ Ⓑ Ⓒ Ⓓ	23 Ⓐ Ⓑ Ⓒ Ⓓ	33 Ⓐ Ⓑ Ⓒ Ⓓ
4 Ⓐ Ⓑ Ⓒ Ⓓ	14 Ⓐ Ⓑ Ⓒ Ⓓ	24 Ⓐ Ⓑ Ⓒ Ⓓ	34 Ⓐ Ⓑ Ⓒ Ⓓ
5 Ⓐ Ⓑ Ⓒ Ⓓ	15 Ⓐ Ⓑ Ⓒ Ⓓ	25 Ⓐ Ⓑ Ⓒ Ⓓ	35 Ⓐ Ⓑ Ⓒ Ⓓ
6 Ⓐ Ⓑ Ⓒ Ⓓ	16 Ⓐ Ⓑ Ⓒ Ⓓ	26 Ⓐ Ⓑ Ⓒ Ⓓ	36 Ⓐ Ⓑ Ⓒ Ⓓ
7 Ⓐ Ⓑ Ⓒ Ⓓ	17 Ⓐ Ⓑ Ⓒ Ⓓ	27 Ⓐ Ⓑ Ⓒ Ⓓ	37 Ⓐ Ⓑ Ⓒ Ⓓ
8 Ⓐ Ⓑ Ⓒ Ⓓ	18 Ⓐ Ⓑ Ⓒ Ⓓ	28 Ⓐ Ⓑ Ⓒ Ⓓ	38 Ⓐ Ⓑ Ⓒ Ⓓ
9 Ⓐ Ⓑ Ⓒ Ⓓ	19 Ⓐ Ⓑ Ⓒ Ⓓ	29 Ⓐ Ⓑ Ⓒ Ⓓ	39 Ⓐ Ⓑ Ⓒ Ⓓ
10 Ⓐ Ⓑ Ⓒ Ⓓ	20 Ⓐ Ⓑ Ⓒ Ⓓ	30 Ⓐ Ⓑ Ⓒ Ⓓ	40 Ⓐ Ⓑ Ⓒ Ⓓ

Sample Test 3

An answer key for this test is on page 249. Explanatory answers begin on page 249.

PART A (15 questions; 10 minutes)

In Part A each problem consists of an incomplete sentence. Four words or phrases, marked (*a*), (*b*), (*c*), (*d*), are given beneath each sentence. You are to choose the one word or phrase that best completes the sentence. Then on your answer sheet, find the number of the problem and mark your answer.

1. I'm not familiar with _____ of computer; please demonstrate it for me.

   (*a*) this kind
   (*b*) these kinds
   (*c*) these kind
   (*d*) this kinds

2. _____ Dan _____ Morley has ever visited Mt. Rushmore.

   (*a*) Neither . . . nor
   (*b*) Either . . . or
   (*c*) Neither . . . or
   (*d*) Either . . . nor

3. They keep telling us that it is vital that we _____ there on time.

   (*a*) were
   (*b*) are
   (*c*) be
   (*d*) to be

4. WNZY-TV was forced off the air because _____

   (*a*) its transmitter broke.
   (*b*) its transmitter had broken.
   (*c*) it broke its transmitter.
   (*d*) its transmitter was broken.

5. The water _____ be very cold at the beach, but the air _____.

    (*a*) isn't . . . is
    (*b*) won't . . . will
    (*c*) won't . . . won't
    (*d*) will . . . will

6. _____ not try to drive on that road in this rainstorm.

    (*a*) She'd better
    (*b*) She'll better
    (*c*) She better'd
    (*d*) She's better

7. Whenever we've needed him _____ always _____ there to help.

    (*a*) he's . . . been
    (*b*) he's . . . being
    (*c*) he'd . . . been
    (*d*) he'll . . . be

8. *War and Peace* was the _____ of the two books we had to read.

    (*a*) most long
    (*b*) longest
    (*c*) more long
    (*d*) longer

9. He decided not to attend the funeral _____ there was a security problem.

    (*a*) due that
    (*b*) because of
    (*c*) due to
    (*d*) because

10. The officer told the recruits that every bit of litter and scrap _____.

    (*a*) were to be picked up
    (*b*) picks up
    (*c*) pick up
    (*d*) was to be picked up

11. Professor Cruickshank always made his classes _____ a term paper.

    (a) to do
    (b) do
    (c) doing
    (d) have to do

12. I think Darryl _____ at 8:15.

    (a) suppose to pick us up
    (b) is supposed to pick us up
    (c) is supposed to be pick us up
    (d) is supposed picking us up

13. Ruby's is, by far, _____ Chinese restaurant in the district.

    (a) the goodest
    (b) the bestest
    (c) the most good
    (d) the best

14. "To dream," the poet said, "it must be better than _____ all one's life."

    (a) groveling
    (b) to grovel
    (c) grovel
    (d) the groveling

15. Chuck won't miss a single Rangers game. _____.

    (a) Neither will I
    (b) Either will I
    (c) Neither won't I
    (d) Either won't I

PART B (25 questions; 15 minutes)

Each problem in Part B consists of a sentence in which four words or phrases are underlined. The four underlined parts of the sentence are marked (*a*), (*b*), (*c*), (*d*). You are to identify the one underlined word or phrase that should be corrected or rewritten. Then on your answer sheet, find the number of the problem and mark your answer.

16. The reason <u>the</u> reporter returned <u>to</u> the scene of the accident
    　　　　　　 a 　　　　　　　　　 *b*

    was <u>because</u> she <u>had forgotten</u> to interview the witness.
    　　　 c 　　　　　　 *d*

17. <u>The</u> unfortunate applicant <u>was</u> ugly, stupid, <u>and</u>
    　 a 　　　　　　　　　　 *b* 　　　　　　　　 *c*

    <u>had no talent.</u>
    　　 d

18. <u>The</u> United States <u>are located</u> in the <u>western</u> hemisphere <u>in</u>
    　 a 　　　　　 *b* 　　　　　　 *c* 　　　　　　 *d*

    North America.

19. <u>The</u> suds from the washing machine <u>has just flowed</u> <u>over</u>
    　 a 　　　　　　　　　　　　　　 *b* 　　　　 *c*

    onto <u>the</u> laundry room floor.
    　　 d

20. Neither management <u>nor</u> the union <u>were</u> happy <u>about</u> the
    　　　　　　　　　 a 　　　　　 *b* 　　　 *c*

    <u>President's</u> wage and price freeze.
    　　 d

21. He <u>said,</u> "You <u>arent</u> the only one <u>who</u> <u>misses</u> the genius of
    　 a 　　　　 *b* 　　　　　 *c* 　 *d*

    John Lennon."

22. You were <u>all together</u> <u>correct</u> in your analysis; <u>these</u> artifacts
    　　　 a 　　　　 *b* 　　　　　　　　 *c*

    are <u>at least</u> 2500 years old.
    　　 d

23. I have been <u>looking</u> <u>at</u> <u>that</u> sailboat, <u>but</u> <u>which</u> is
    　　　　　　 a 　 *b* 　　　　　　 *c*

    <u>too expensive</u> for me.
    　　 d

---

24. "Rafael, will you please do this chore as I asked you to?"
                               a   *b*   *c*

    "Yes, I will do."
            d

25. If either of the two samples turn out to be radioactive, we'll
                                    a   *b*

    have to turn them in to the proper authorities.
       c   *d*

26. I'm not certain, but I don't think we have some of that par-
           a   *b*

    ticular brand in stock just now.
              c   *d*

27. The baby chickens are so young that I don't think either can
                      a   *b*

    stand on their own feet without falling.
          c   *d*

28. The clerk called the meeting to order, and the minutes of the
                     a   *b*   *c*

    previous meeting were read.
            d

29. Chuck has been promised me some action on my proposal
             a   *b* *c*

    for months.
      d

30. This painting needs to be reframing before we can hang it in
    a   *b*   *c*   *d*

    the gallery.

31. The border guard commanded the truck stop to be searched
                a   *b*   *c*

    for contraband.
    d

32. We cheered the beating team, even though they lost
      a   *b*   *c*

    ignominiously.
      d

33. I've learned <u>much</u> valuable things <u>just</u> <u>by watching</u> that car-
         a   b   c
penter <u>work</u>.
        d

34. I think the store <u>is closed</u>; we can always buy
                              a
<u>tomorrow morning</u> the film <u>you want</u> <u>for</u> your camera.
        b   c   d

35. The article <u>says</u> <u>that</u> Africans eat <u>more</u> peanuts than
                   a   b   c
<u>South Americans</u>.
        d

36. We won't be able to travel <u>in</u> Amtrak from Chicago to
                                  a
Denver <u>anymore</u>; <u>they're</u> discontinuing <u>rail service</u>.
           b   c   d

37. The chef explained <u>where</u> he was going <u>to add</u> the wine to the
                           a   b
coq au vin <u>at</u> the <u>very last</u> moment.
              c   d

38. The <u>real</u> cause of high unemployment <u>in</u> our state <u>is</u> <u>jobs</u>.
            a   b   c   d

39. The Pope's journeys <u>have taken</u> <u>him</u> to the Philippines,
                            a   b
Poland, Brazil, <u>and</u> <u>to</u> Nigeria.
                   c   d

40. *Cat's Cradle* and *Mother Night* <u>is</u> what propelled Kurt
                                         a
Vonnegut <u>into</u> national prominence <u>as</u> a <u>first-rate</u> novelist.
             b   c   d

STOP! End of Sample Test 3

Sample Test 3: Answer Key

1. *a*	11. *b*	21. *b*	31. *b*
2. *a*	12. *b*	22. *a*	32. *b*
3. *c*	13. *d*	23. *c*	33. *a*
4. *d*	14. *b*	24. *d*	34. *b*
5. *b*	15. *a*	25. *a*	35. *d*
6. *a*	16. *c*	26. *b*	36. *a*
7. *a*	17. *d*	27. *c*	37. *a*
8. *d*	18. *b*	28. *d*	38. *d*
9. *d*	19. *b*	29. *a*	39. *d*
10. *d*	20. *b*	30. *b*	40. *a*

Sample Test 3: Explanatory Answers

The numbers in parentheses refer to the rules covering each point.

1. (*a*) Only (*a*) is acceptable. The pronoun *it* in the second clause tells us that the term is singular. Choice (*b*) is plural; (*c*) and (*d*) are grammatically unacceptable in any circumstance. (**33; 34**)

2. (*a*) Only (*a*) is acceptable. The use of *ever* requires a negative correlative conjunction. Choice (*b*) is positive; (*c*) and (*d*) are grammatically unacceptable in any circumstance. (**197**)

3. (*c*) Only (*c*) is acceptable. The subjunctive mood uses *be* throughout the present tense. Choice (*a*) is past; (*b*) and (*d*) are improper forms for the subjunctive. (**63**)

4. (*d*) The best choice is (*d*). The main clause verb is passive voice, past tense; thus, the dependent clause verb should be in the same voice and tense. Choices (*a*) and (*c*) are active voice; (*b*) is past perfect tense. (**71; 86**)

5. (*b*) Only (*b*) is acceptable. The structure of the sentence requires a contrast (*but*); thus, if the first verb is negative, the second must be affirmative. Choices (*c*) and (*d*) don't contrast; (*a*) is grammatically unacceptable. (**96**)

6. (*a*) Only (*a*) is acceptable. *Had better* is an auxiliary verb that expresses advisability. (**103**)

7. (*a*) Only (*a*) is acceptable. The present perfect tense is appropriate in sentences that indicate that an action has been repeated several times in the past. The other choices use the wrong tense. (**77c**)

8. (*d*) Only (*d*) is acceptable. One-syllable adjectives that are used to compare two items form their comparative degree by adding -*er*. Choice (*b*) is superlative; (*a*) and (*c*) are improper forms of comparison. (**157; 159; 160**)

9. (*d*) Only (*d*) is acceptable. An adverbial clause should be introduced by a conjunctive adverb. Choice (*c*) introduces adjectival clauses; (*a*) and (*b*) are unacceptable forms. (**131**)

10. (*d*) When *every* modifies a subject, the predicate is singular, as it is in (*d*). Choice (*a*) is plural; (*b*) and (*c*) are active voice, unacceptable in this passive voice sentence. (**251**)

11. (*b*) Only the simple form of the verb may be used after *make*. (**122**)

12. (*b*) Only (*b*) uses the correct form of the verb to express expectation; namely, *be supposed to* + the simple form of the verb. (**109**)

13. (*d*) Choice (*d*) is the correct superlative form of *good*; none of the other choices are grammatically acceptable in any circumstance. (**165**)

14. (*b*) Only (*b*) uses parallel construction to complete the comparison ("To dream . . . to grovel . . . ."). (**231**)

15. (*a*) Only (*a*) is an acceptable rejoinder for this sentence; it is modeled on the preceding statement. (**98**)

16. (*c*) A reason cannot be *because*. Thus, "The reason . . . was that she had forgotten . . . ." (**226**)

17. (*d*) The pattern in this sentence is subject + verb + predicate adjective + predicate adjective. Then, instead of an expected third predicate adjective, there is a clause. The principle of parallelism demands a third predicate adjective: ". . . was ugly, stupid, and untalented." (**231**)

18. (*b*) Countries are singular even if their names appear to be plural; thus, the U.S. is singular, requiring a singular verb: "The United States is located . . . ." (**3; 242**)

19. (*b*) *Suds* is a plural noun that requires a plural verb: "The suds . . . have just flowed over . . . ." (**4; 245**)

20. (*b*) When a compound subject is joined by *nor*, the predicate agrees with the nearer subject. *Union* is a collective noun used singularly; thus, the predicate must also be singular: ". . . nor the union was happy about . . . ." (**247**)

21. (*b*) The correct contraction for *are not* is *aren't*. (**91; 258**)

22. (*a*) *All together* means "all in one place or group"; *altogether* means "wholly" or "entirely." Thus, "You were altogether correct . . . ." An *artifact* is an item made by humans, usually a tool or device of historical interest. (Usage **15**)

23. (c) A coordinate conjunction is inappropriate in this sentence since one thought depends on the other. Thus, "I have been looking at that sailboat which is too expensive for me" or "That sailboat I have been looking at is too expensive for me" or "I have been looking at that sailboat; however, it is too expensive for me." (227; 228)

24. (d) Short answers are formed by adding *yes* or *no* + a pronoun + the auxiliary verb used in the question (but not the main verb). Thus, "Yes, I will." (95)

25. (a) *Either* is a singular pronoun subject that requires a singular verb. *Samples* is not the subject; it is the object of the preposition *of*. Thus, "If either of the two samples turns out to be . . . ." (35)

26. (b) *Some* is used in affirmative statements; *any* is used in negative statements: ". . . don't think we have any of that . . . ." *Just now* is an idiom meaning "at this time." (40)

27. (c) The antecedent of the possessive pronoun is *either*. Even though we are clearly talking about a plural noun (*chickens*), the structure considers each individually by using the singular indefinite pronoun *either*; thus, its pronoun reference should also be singular: ". . . either can stand on its own feet . . . ." (49)

28. (d) There is no reason for the shift from the active voice to the passive voice: "The clerk called the meeting to order and read the minutes of the last meeting." To *call to order* means "request that people be quiet and attentive." *Minutes* are official records of the proceedings at the meetings of organizations. (71)

29. (a) Actions that begin in the past and continue up to the present are expressed by either the present perfect tense or the present perfect progressive tense: "Chuck has promised me some . . . ." or "Chuck has been promising me some . . . ." (77; 84)

30. (b) *Needs to be* requires a past participle to express necessity: "This painting needs to be reframed before we . . . ." Another possibility is: "This painting needs reframing before we . . . ." (111)

31. (b) When *command* is followed by a verb, it must be an infinitive: ". . . commanded the truck to stop to be searched . . . ." (123)

32. (b) The proper form of this adjective is the past participle of *beat*, not the present participle; the past participle shows that the noun received the action: "We cheered the beaten team . . . ." *Ignominiously* means "humiliatingly" or "disgracefully." (134)

33. (a) *Much* is used with noncountable nouns; *many* is used with countable nouns: "I've learned many valuable things . . . ." (145)

34. (*b*) Adverbs of time should be placed at the beginning or at the end of a clause, and they should never separate verbs from their direct objects. Thus, "... we can always buy the film you want for your camera tomorrow morning." (**154; 156**)

35. (*d*) This comparison is misleading; it seems to say that Africans eat South Americans, not that they eat peanuts more frequently. The sentence should read: "... eat more peanuts than South Americans do." (**168**)

36. (*a*) One travels *on* a train or *by* train: "... be able to travel on Amtrak from ...." or "... be able to travel by Amtrak from ...." The term *rail service* means "railroad or train activity." (**190**)

37. (*a*) *Where* introduces adverbial clauses; the subordinate clause in this sentence is a noun clause; thus, *where* cannot introduce it: "The chef explained that he was ...." *Coq au vin* is a chicken dish prepared with red wine, brandy, mushrooms, and onions. (**212; 213**)

38. (*d*) This is illogical; jobs cannot be the cause of no jobs. The sentence needs a new conclusion in order to make logical sense. Examples would be: "The real cause ... is a faltering economy." or "The real cause ... is the government's tax policy." (**224**)

39. (*d*) The preposition should not be repeated in this construction: "... to the Philippines, Poland, Brazil, and Nigeria." It would also be acceptable, however, to repeat the preposition before each country: "... to the Philippines, to Poland, to Brazil, and to Nigeria." (**230**)

40. (*a*) When two or more subjects are joined by *and*, the predicate is plural: "*Cat's Cradle* and *Mother Night* are what propelled ...." (**246**)